stumbling tow...

my longing to heal from the evil that God allowed

renée altson

foreword by phyllis tickle

Stumbling Toward Faith
Copyright © 2004 by Youth Specialties

Youth Specialties Books, 300 South Pierce Street, El Cajon, CA 92020, are published by
Zondervan, 5300 Patterson Avenue SE, Grand Rapids, MI 49530

Library of Congress Cataloging-in-Publication Data

Altson, Renee, 1969-
  Stumbling toward faith : my longing to heal from the evil that God allowed / by Renee
Altson.
     p. cm.
  ISBN 0-310-25755-7 (softcover)
  1. Altson, Renee, 1969- 2. Christian biography--United States. I. Title.
  BR1725.A655A3 2004
    277.3'082'092--dc22

                                                                        2004008753

Unless otherwise indicated, all Scripture quotations are taken from the Holy Bible: New
International Version (North American Edition). Copyright © 1973, 1978, 1984 by
International Bible Society. Used by permission of Zondervan.

Some of the anecdotal illustrations in this book are true to life and are included with the
permission of the persons involved. All other illustrations are composites of real situations,
and any resemblance to people living or dead is coincidental.

Web site addresses listed in this book were current at the time of publication. Please contact
Youth Specialties via e-mail (YS@YouthSpecialties.com) to report URLs that are no longer
operational and replacement URLs if available.

Editing and project direction by Dave Urbanski
Cover and interior design by Proxy
Printed in the United States of America

04 05 06 07 08 09 / DC / 10 9 8 7 6 5 4 3 2 1

for the "little mother" who gave me life,
and eric & jordan who give me joy.

foreword

what you are about to read is an experience captured in a book. like some kind of chimera, that experience is pinioned here just long enough for you and me to stare at it, as if through a brief freeze-frame in time. then, almost beyond our knowing, it breaks loose of us and is free again, so free that we question whether our presence ever really interrupted its flight. if we are honest, we question as well whether any one of us can ever really comprehend its outlines, much less discern its intricacies.

this is the first work from an immensely gifted young writer from whom, pray god, we will receive many, many more words marshaled to her strange beat and through whom, pray god, we will gain purchase over many more demons and wild things, caught momentarily in her verbal lens.

this is a love story, credible and grand as few love stories are, because this one is so understated and so lately inserted as almost to be assumed. before it is done, this is also a mother's story, also slyly inserted.

this is a cautionary tale for all those who presume to counsel the young or even presume to live feckless near those places that nurture them.

this is a horror story as well, though it has no resolution, being far too honest for such easy disposition. that is to say, this is a published report of personal damage that cannot be undone and that, in the end, must be acknowledged as present by all of us who are of the religion in which it happened.

this book is an accusation, though it is not so much meanly delivered as matter-of-factly articulated. it simply acknowledges that the stumbling blocks of dogma used to build renée altson's charnel house were quarried by a christian establishment more organized than holy, but which was and is, by name at least, still our establishment. it without ceremony shows that the gruel of clichés used to starve her into submission came from the kitchens of christian institutions more human than inspired, but which were and are, by name at least, still our institutions.

stumbling toward faith is all of these things—and to categorize it as only any one of them without categorizing it as all is to eviscerate it. but this book is one other thing as well: it is a proto-myth...a piece of poetry in transit. it is the autobiography of the phoenix retold in today's circumstances, but still emerging from cruel fires.

the question this book does not answer, of course, is how each of us christians must respond since, by grace, we have been allowed to witness the phoenix rising.

that one is up to us.

phyllis tickle
the farm in lucy
easter 2004

introduction

my birth name always felt alien to me. it was difficult to pronounce, difficult to spell, and i was named after someone i never really wanted to be. that's why, at a crucial point in my counseling, i asked my therapist if he would be willing to rename me.

he was honored and spent some time in the baby section of a local bookstore, looking up meanings and definitions, his eyes growing bleary with the choices. a few sessions later, he handed it to me somewhat anticlimactically on a sheet of paper:

renée.

i am able to write this book partly because that is my new name. i haven't used any of my birth names for years. they've all been legally changed, written over with a new arrangement of vowels and consonants, scrubbed clean of any association with the past. it was a bit like coming back to life again, being given that new name. it meant a fresh start, a new chance, a hope of finding myself brave after many years of fear and trembling.

—renée altson (renee@stumblingtowardfaith.com)

stumbling toward faith

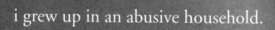
i grew up in an abusive household.

much of my abuse was spiritual—and when i say spiritual, i don't mean new age, esoteric, random mumblings from half-wiccan, hippie parents. i don't mean that i grew up thinking all the wrong ideas about religion or what it meant to be saved because i was given too much freedom or too many options. i don't mean that my father protested the phrase "under god" in the pledge of allegiance or told me there was more than one way to heaven.

i mean that my father raped me while reciting the lord's prayer.

i mean that my father molested me while singing christian hymns. i mean that there was one way, that i was (literally) "under god," and that i could never escape my sinfulness.

never.

my father corrupted nearly every single thing that in my deepest moments of belief i see that god created for good or for righteousness.

he did it slyly, without my even realizing it.

he did it deliberately, without regret.

he fully convinced me that god was on his side, that i was bad, that i was lucky to be loved (by god, by him, by anyone), and that i was to blame for things no child—nobody—should ever be blamed for.

i had a strange sense of power because of this. i was terrified of god, yet i felt more powerful than god at the same time. my dad told me that if the sun didn't come out in the morning, it was because it (the sun) "didn't want to look at your ugly face."

so i felt more powerful than the sun, but i felt powerless under the weight of my father's body.

i made wagers but never followed through on my agreements.

i dared god to kill me (it would have been a welcome relief). i embraced fundamentalism—it was familiar, it fit in with my self-blame, and to some extent, my overblown sense of power.

i wandered through various religions, particularly the ones with strict rules and definitive boundaries. i was baptized a mormon, a jehovah's witness. i flirted with scientology. in the end, i came to one conclusion: the warm acceptance i felt in each of these groups was only there because i was conforming to that group's ideals. the people only loved me because they had to, because it was written in their religion that they treat others well. they only had faith in me because i shared their faith, too.

the moment i doubted, or strayed, or showed independence, they became vultures. they told me i was unworthy. it was almost like living with my father all over again. almost.

i don't even know what "home" means, except that i long for it. i long to heal, to have this yawning chasm inside of me filled, to believe in something bigger than me, holier than i dare to imagine, more gracious and full of kindness than i dare to wish for.

this book is an expression

of my journey "home."

a dusty cathedral inside my heart:
cobwebs engulfing a silent altar,
hardened wax from a burned-out soul.

i don't know when the beauty died,
or when the breath of god grew stale
or how the candles
—monuments of glory—
were consumed
and engulfed
by the darkness.

down on my knees in the rubble
surrounded by fragments
of shattered stained glass
cutting,
ripping,
slashing tender skin.

collections of teardrops
in bottles and bell jars,
skipping a stone, for every sin.

my father prayed with me every night.

he lay on top of me, touched my breasts, and prayed that i would be forgiven.

"father," he said.

i cringed at the association.

"heavenly father, make my daughter a better person.

let her be good enough for her mother to come back. let her prove to her mother that she is a good girl. we know that her mother left because she was a bad girl. help her to be good enough. make her a better person. take away her sin. forgive her in spite of how awful she is. let your blood cover all her sin. help her to stop being so bad."

i lay underneath him and trembled. i closed my eyes, as much to avoid his face as to pray properly. i made promises. to stop disappointing him, to stop disappointing god. i repented for all my sins, for all of my wrongdoings, admitted my fallen wretchedness, my guilt, my shame.

i would have done anything to bring my mother back.

i would have done anything to feel clean, feel loved, to have been good.

a white-skinned virgin
lies naked and ashamed
on the altar of your madness.
obsessed with the purity
of a never-broken heart,
of a never-broken child,
so perfect,
so ripe for the taking.

our consecrated rite:
in and out
pounding in the soul,
pleading in the heart,
    (helpmehelpmehelpmehelpmehelpmeholdme)

lying open on your altar
paralyzed
helpless
disbelieving.

where is the sacrifice, father?
where is the ram in the thicket?

i am the ram.
i am the sacrifice.
the only thing good enough for god.
for you.

i drove through the darkened streets, crying so hard the wheel vibrated underneath my hands. i didn't dare pull over; i was afraid the grief and shame would destroy me, that it would make me stiff, that i'd slip away.

i had just left my associate pastor's office. he was a man i'd deeply admired—the first one after years at the wrong church who had won my confidence, my trust. we'd met a couple of times, and at the time he said he liked me. he told me i was a sensitive soul, that god would do great things in my life.

i believed him. i forced myself to. i had spent years seeking great things for my life, great movements of god, emotional healing, a sense of purpose, connection. i didn't want to be the one who never had miracles, the one who always sat on the god sidelines while everybody else got god touchdowns.

the summer mission trip was part of those god dreams.

i wanted to go to mongolia. there was so much sadness there, so much brokenness. i believed, just by looking at photos of those folks, that god would do great things for them. they had hunger in their eyes, the same quiet but desperate longing i saw in my own. i believed somehow that, by offering god to them, i would find god offered back to me as well.

i filled out the mission trip application at a jack in the box restaurant. drinking a strawberry shake, and with trembling hands, i answered all the questions. how long i'd been saved, what jesus meant to me, why i wanted to go share the good news.

then i got to the page devoted to "what is god doing in your life?" and i realized, with regret, that i didn't know what to say. god had been pretty silent for me; he hadn't given me a whole lot of touchdowns. i still believed in him (i still wanted to believe). i still saw how he gave to other people. i saw their changed lives. i saw their moments, their miracles. and i still yearned for that kind of obvious divine intervention.

and my associate pastor had promised it would come. i wanted to believe i wasn't beyond its reach.

so, in that jack in the box, with '80s music blaring and teenagers smoking pot right outside the back door,

i wrote the truth: "i believe god is calling me to this mission trip because this is part of what he wants to do in my life.

i have felt stale and old and tired. i have wanted to rediscover god, even as i am sharing the discovery of him with others. i understand the desperation of wanting god and not being able to find him, i share that desperation still. i want to find god in mongolia."

a few weeks later an adult volunteer pulled me aside after a midweek meeting.

"hey," he said, avoiding my eyes.

i looked directly at him, dared him to look back.
he didn't.

"we've reviewed your application for the mongolia trip and decided you can't go."

i stood there in disbelief, questions and thoughts flitting through my head. "i can't go? can't go? isn't a mission trip something that everybody can go on? isn't a mission trip, by simple definition, something that everybody should want to do? share the good news? change the world? isn't it some kind of sin to say that somebody can't go?"

i tried to understand it. it couldn't have been about

money—i had to arrange my own support; the church offered nothing more than the schedule and the contacts. it couldn't have been about the number of people applying, i knew that there were more spots than there were people even interested.

tears filled my eyes, and i stammered out the question: "wh-wh-why?"

"we need people who are confident in their faith. we need people who are committed. you are not confident, you are not committed. i'm sorry," he said, patting my shoulder. "maybe next year."

i ran out of the building and toward the haven of my associate pastor's office. he would understand. he would know. he had promised great things for me. he had believed in me—in god in me. he had promised that god would work in me, and he would know that this was part of that working, part of the promise.

but when my associate pastor saw me coming, he shook his head sadly, stood up from his desk, and closed the door while i was still at the other end of the hallway. i wanted to pound on the door. i wanted to fling myself through it, into his office, to plead for another chance, to prove my worthiness. instead i stood in the middle of the room, frozen with horror, and felt the shame overwhelm me. tears ran down my cheeks, burning as they fell. i was engulfed in nausea. i felt myself stop breathing.

the repulsion that god must have felt for me welled up inside. my shame encompassed me. "i am not good enough to do the work of god," i thought. "i am not good enough for him to use me. there is something inside me that even god can never touch, can never change."

i ran out to the parking lot, past the clusters of other college students having cookies and coffee while discussing amy grant's backsliding. i opened the car door, sat down in the seat, and started driving, aimlessly, afraid to stop, afraid to be left alone with myself, alone with my feelings of self-loathing and self-hatred, alone with my sense of self-revulsion.

driving around in the car that night i played the song "when god ran" by benny hester over and over, sobbing through the words, screaming out like a prodigal, begging god to take me back: "the day i left home i knew i'd broken his heart / i wondered then if things could ever be the same..."

i confessed every little thing i could think of. i apologized over and over for my wickedness, my unbelief; i made deals and bargains with god. and in the end, after several hours and many miles, i pulled up in front of my father's house, opened the car door, and realized that what was wrong with me was unchangeable.

my whole life my father said i was beyond hope, that in the end no one would ever love me. he had said god could never trust me, that i would never be clean, that

i would never be good enough.

i believed him. and now i understood why.

the church officially agreed.

i've spent my life believing i have nothing to offer god. certainly he died for me, and my worth exists so far as he was willing to redeem me, to make me his child. if i were the only person on earth he would have still gone to the cross, and all of that. but me, the person i am apart from god, apart from grace, is worthless without him.

it wasn't just the fear of hell that kept me on the floor by my bed, kneeling, begging to be born again.

it was the fear of being worthless, of being lost, of being unloved. i was terrified of my horrible sin nature, terrified it would devour me, strangle my life, swallow my potential.

there was little separation between god and self, and what distinction i could find was based on outcome. if i did well on a test, even if i had studied, i gave god the glory. if i failed a test, even if i had studied, it was that i hadn't tried hard enough. the only way to do well, to be well, was to replace myself with god.

when my associate pastor was asked how he was, he'd reply, "happier than i'm entitled, praise god."

i never understood these things, but i believed them. they ingrained themselves into my heart and helped define the way i saw myself, all that i was apart from the mercy of god.

i sit in the darkness
waiting with clenched fists
for the light.

i always knew something was terribly wrong with my place in god's world. i constantly longed for something bigger than me, bigger than the religion i saw all around me, something that had no words, though i tried to define it with words.

in desperation i raced toward things that pretended to ease the loneliness, the aching yearning broken emptiness i could never explain. i swallowed offered solutions without argument, though they tasted bitter, though i wondered if they were poison even as they went down.

the cathartic release that followed "inner healing" or deliverance sessions gave me a sense of wholeness, a connection to some kind of temporary superpower, a conviction of resolution. after many hours crying, sweating, pleading the name of jesus, banishing evil thoughts and casting out spirits, i could sleep again. my self-hatred diminished. my head cleared. i thought i felt love.

but when the pain, struggle, and doubt returned, it swept me under its power, and i found myself overwhelmed, feeling helpless, unloved, unvalued, and unsaved. all the "truths" that came to me in those powerful moments of "inner healing" had vanished from my consciousness. all my worth in god's eyes dissipated, and i was left struggling for conviction that i mattered, convicted only of my brokenness, my terror, and my shame.

the people praying over me didn't know what to do with me. i frustrated them. i was able to tolerate my thoughts and felt somewhat accepted insofar as they saw me as clean, swept out, freshly prayed over and confessed, but once real life crashed into me, and the despair presented itself to them as raw, vulnerable woundedness, they feared for my salvation and their own expectations of christianity were threatened.

my pain didn't fit into their carefully prescribed solutions, their falsely created illusions of "what god does" and "who god is." my questions, my despair, my broken stilted half-destroyed faith wasn't good enough for their pat answers and had no place among them. they wanted a god who changed lives, who eliminated doubt and fear, who was greater than any situation, any person's pain.

so i was a failure. i wasn't living the right christian life. i wasn't doing enough, praying enough, trying enough. the shame, the confusion, the longing, the failing was mine, for "god is not a god of confusion," and "god is incapable of failure."

then i learned how to pretend. i learned how to define my relationship with the supernatural with words that minimized and limited it. i began to limit myself, to define who i was with an expected predictability and with the smallest definitions.

the pretending felt real…sometimes.

i welcomed my non-thinking, my ability to escape from my pain. i embraced their answers and buried my doubt and insecurity so deeply that i could deny it was ever there. but when the hollow emptiness of my spirituality crashed into me, when i was alone with my lingering discontent, i was disillusioned with what i thought was my faith. it had no lasting solutions, nothing that wasn't based on pretenses. it had no real depth.

and when the time came to open my hands and show my christianity, i discovered i was clutching nothing. my grip was empty. my belief was shallow. my pain was buried beneath a facade that only looked good on the outside.

now, as i try to find my faith, as i try to find my spirituality, i struggle to understand who i really am, who i have been, who i was in those restless years. i am struggling to understand god apart from the words i used, the words i placed on my christianity in order to belong, to fit in, to survive. take the words away, and i am lost.

there are many layers to my story,
to all of these words,
this lostness.

i tell as much as i can,
with the words that i have,
and still i feel the fracture of the partial,
still i feel the emptiness of the untold.

holiness tugs at my mind. the seduction of being forgiven, a way to know i'm accepted.

holiness is a familiar siren's song: it's the only thing that will save you, they always said. the only way you will ever, can ever, be complete, put back together again, they said.

holiness was my promised elixir to happiness, the unquestioning, undeniable conviction of being right with god, the certainty of obedience. holiness was proof: i have changed, i am good, i am loved.

but it was always about how terrible i was, my blackness, my dirty disgusting filth, all that made me unlovable and unsaveable, all that made me headed toward death—a death i was always told i deserved.

even repentance wasn't enough. penitence, naked and beaten, apologies and humiliation; it was never enough. my sins were always so much bigger, my shame so much greater. i often wished they would leave me a sinner; that they would leave me alone.

even so, they said, christ didn't even want to forgive me or love me—he had to, he was called to, he was driven to. it was his job, those sweats of blood, that bent up, shriveled posture in the garden, that quiet surrender, the way he held back peter's sword, he'd come just for that purpose, just for those moments. he was (as those christmas cards said) born to die.

in high school, sitting in class, i doodled on my history notes, on my algebra test: me too, born to die. i wished for an escape—for my own end, for my own nothingness, for some kind of redemption at the conclusion of it all.

all of those years of church, of easter dresses, of screaming on the kitchen chair as chunks of my hair were brushed out, pulled, knots untangled, a pile of rebellious strands on the floor.

i remember my long blue dress. it was like air, it floated on me, it had white polka dots. i remember my white sandals—and an order to keep them out of the mud. i remember the red construction-paper cross i made on my bedroom wall, so desperate i was to be forgiven, to be holy, to have my evil scrubbed away. furtive scribbling of cryptic sins on torn shreds of notebook paper, taped to the cross so i'd remember them; the red was completely covered. i'd rip it all down easter morning, passionately, with tears and hot angry breathing: i'm free, i'm free, he can't punish me for these things anymore.

but forgiveness, the blood of christ, easter, it was never enough for my father. it began again, the next moment, the next breath: too many doubts, not enough christian love, too much disrespect, selfishness, greed. all of that forgiveness meant nothing.nothing. that brief fleeting second of suddenly being okay and clean and acceptable was flushed away, deleted.

as it is written,
there is no one righteous,
not even one…
all have turned away,
they have together become worthless…

romans 3:10,12

how can i reconcile the pain and sadness of the past

to this present moment, to this overwhelming feeling, this certainty: i am not good enough. i am never good enough.

how do i find strength when it feels like i am weaker than i have ever been? can i find joy in small moments of progress, in small moments of learning to simply be?

if i dare to embrace my sorrow, if i dare to acknowledge my broken faith, will i find that i am holding nothing? that the faith i seek comes only to those who are put-together, pretending, and whole? if i reach into these dark corners of my soul searching for treasure, for purpose, will my hands come up empty?

is this loss i feel part of what i have given away? these ingrained definitions, these lifelong limitations; i have thrown them off in search of a bigger god, in search of a bigger version of me. what if there is nothing beyond what i have?

i tremble for all i cannot hold, for all that i cannot reach.

i have such tremendous longing in me, such tremendous shame.

i wear this shame like a second skin,

a constant presence. in each moment i second-guess myself, question my sincerity, question my worth.

how can i believe that i am loved, truly loved, as long as i feel in that same breath that i am absolutely worthless?

what is the line between believing that i am a sinner saved by grace and believing that i am adored and beloved of god? how can i begin to find a connection with my worth in the eyes of god when i am drowning in what i was told about who i am, what i am, when i see myself through my own eyes as incapable of being loved?

it was easy for the church, for my father, to write definitions on me. they had years of patriarchy, a conviction of the second-class status of women, with original sin and the fall itself backing them up. i wore the shame my father placed upon me because i couldn't escape it, and the church heaped even more on top of that, never realizing that what i needed to know, more than anything, was that i was loved, that i was beloved, that i was precious enough to god to be purchased, to be chosen, to be light.

it became a relentless cycle,

a depression i couldn't escape. it became a constant presence. my impression of the holy spirit became synonymous with feeling evil, with feeling never good enough. the conviction of the spirit was the conviction of my horrible worthlessness.

i thought it was the way i was supposed to feel.

they defined me and classified me and told me who i was without ever really knowing me.

nobody ever told me i could genuinely matter to god.

wednesday nights were always made up of the committed ones, the serious ones—the kids who really burned with passion for the right thing, for god.

we got there, rushed from school and study labs and band practice, our hair tangled, our clothes mussed. we grabbed some fast food dinner on the way or gulped down something around the family table while finishing our homework. we ran down the stairs, thumping our arrival, smacking our bubble gum all the way to the church library.

there was always an element of gossip about our midweek bible studies. we were scattered around the county, so midweek was the perfect time to talk about our respective schools: who won what football game, how we placed in the semifinals, did you see that so-and-so was chosen for the scholarship?

as a group we worked through some kind of christian teen book, i hardly remember it now. one thing it did have, and something our associate pastor stressed, was daily devotional readings, personal reflections, and "homework."

we were supposed to spend a little bit of time each day "in the word"—exactly 1 hour and 3 scripture verses and 5 little questions. "apply it to your daily life," they said. "get in the habit of spending daily time with the lord—it's the most important thing you can do as a christian. it's the only way you can hear his voice, it's the only way to really know that you're following him."

one wednesday evening, as we giggled among ourselves, the associate pastor strode into the room, the air growing colder with his very presence.

"we are starting something new next week," he said. "you'll

read all four gospels and answer questions about them.
spend time with the lord, and if you miss a
day, let your work be unfinished."

he walked back up the stairs toward the bathrooms and the
chatting began again.

weeks came and went. we started our new assignment, and i
didn't do it more often than i did. still, i'd thought seriously
about the gospels and tried to be honest in my personal
reflection time. i answered the questions with a smidgen
of vulnerability and a lot of contemplation. i was proud of
what i'd done (probably a little too proud, in fact).

but when i ran down the stairs into the library, i'd see
a cluster of kids copying each other's answers. i'd see
them making up lost days and escaped moments, writing
variations on each other's themes. they didn't even read
the scripture passages. instead it was a snapshot out of 7th
period english: "psst—what did you get for number 4? what
did the verses tell you in number 2?"

i'd roll my eyes, and (truthfully) i'd
feel a little self-righteous that i wasn't
participating. in some ways, it was a
badge of honor that i wasn't cheating,
that i was following my associate pastor's
advice—his pointed directions, after all.

months went by, and we completed the study. a service was
planned for the next sunday: the choir would sing, a few
of the kids would testify about our latest mission trip, and
some of us would talk about reading the four gospels. we
were warned that we would be called on unexpectedly, with

no warning, so we should be prepared to talk about our experiences.

the sunday night arrived, and i sat with my father in my blue checked little house on the prairie gingham choir dress (we were baptists; we didn't have robes). we sang our music (an amy grant medley, an old-time gospel camp-meeting song, and a michael w. smith tune), we testified, and we listened to the associate pastor preach the evening sermon.

he opened his bible with flair, read a passage from the new testament, looked above his bifocal glasses, and said, "i'd like the following kids to come up here when i call their names." he called the names of kids in my bible study. "bobby, andrea, ned, trisha…" he went through every name but mine. soon everyone in the entire bible study was standing at the front of the church.

everyone but me.

"these folks have all done a very important thing," my associate pastor continued. "they have all finished their bible assignments with flying colors."

he described a little bit of the study, talked about the "do it every day" rule, and praised the kids for their hard work and their dedication.

and then he talked about me.

"renée was the only one who did not do this," he said. "let us pray for her and her commitment to god."

i wanted the roof to fall down and crush me. it's an understatement to say that for years after that, every time i walked through the door of that sanctuary, i felt the shame, the horror, the humiliation of that one frozen moment.

and then the associate pastor, in front of 100 people and a line of "good" students, prayed for me.

my father's hand on my thigh was heavy and threatening.

my face burned. tears filled up behind my eyes. i dared not let them fall.

"we pray for renée's repentance, for her dedication ..."

i wanted to run away, but there was nowhere to go. i knew if i left i could never, ever come back.

"we pray for her relationship with you, her commitment to you..."

some part of me did run away and never come back, though, some part of me sitting there on that pew, in that church, on that day, many years ago.

i'm looking for her, for that wounded, shamed long-lost part of me, but i don't know her name.

oh god that is bigger than me.
oh god that is bigger than
daily devotionals,
perfect answers
and unholy pretending.

i believe.
i want to believe.
be present in the depths

of my unbelief.

i grew up a woman in a world that doesn't really value women.

we were nothing more than accessories, depositories for aggression, child-raisers and potluck chefs and housekeepers. our primary purpose in life, as christians, was to "glorify god." our primary purpose in life, as women, was to "glorify god by serving men."

i never felt valued in my church, and it mirrored the environment in my home; in fact, my father took advantage of my christian worthlessness and magnified and manipulated it for his use. to be a woman at church was to be submissive, to not question men, to wear dresses, and to behave properly. i was told that having a will of my own was not allowed, that a voice of my own was not permitted— everything that was allowed as a part of me came through my father. he spoke for my voicelessness, took the credit for my triumphs, and explained away my individuality.

in the darkest moments of my abuse, my father reminded me of my worthlessness in the eyes of god.

he reminded me of my worthlessness in the eyes of the church. and i, feeling small and powerless and abused, felt his words bounce around in my emptiness and finally lodge in the depths of who i was, in the very fabric of my self.

i have grown up believing that i am nothing. i have grown up believing that my worth exists only as much as the men in my life deem me worthy.

god
i seek
validation
evidence
that i matter
to you

sometimes when the flashback pain comes, i try to reason that it must have been so much worse for jesus. the way he gasped for breath, the beating, the agony of the thorns. the aches in my own body remind me of the one who suffered for me, the one whose suffering was amplified so much in my evangelical upbringing that ultimately it was meaningless.

they walked through, in explicit detail, every moment of his suffering. the passion. all that he did "out of love for you." they read quotes from christian doctors and defined every last wound, every implication of every strike. evidence that demands a verdict, they said—see how much he endured, see how much he bore on his own body, in his own skin?

i, in my own abuse, replied "me too." i know that pain, or part of that pain. at the same time, the sexual abuse—the ripping out and violating of my womanhood—was something i felt he didn't understand. my associate pastor told me that god understood everything, that he became as we are so that we might know he was one of us.

i protested quietly, in my own heart: but he was not a woman. he had no idea what it was like to be female in a male world. he had no idea what it felt like to be raped, to have no will.

and they never brought it up. did the male church leaders, in all of their maleness, even think of it? even as they said the words, "he knows what it's like, yet without sin," did they ever consider that maybe he didn't? and if i even mentioned a hint of it, they minimized it entirely. "yes, dear, he understands you," they said, patting the top of my head and shooing me out the door.

it was a remote understanding—the kind of understanding that meant something because it encompassed everything somehow. it may not have been that exact situation, they said, but he knows the general feeling. he knows loss, grief, despair, sorrow. he knows everything; he knows your pain.

i nodded, bore my father's weight in silence, and cried myself to sleep feeling misunderstood and alone.

then they came to jericho. as jesus and his disciples, together with a large crowd, were leaving the city, a blind man, bartimaeus (that is, the son of timaeus), was sitting by the roadside begging. when he heard that it was jesus of nazareth, he began to shout, "jesus, son of david, have mercy on me!"

many rebuked him and told him to be quiet, but he shouted all the more, "son of david, have mercy on me!"

jesus stopped and said, "call him." so they called to the blind man, "cheer up! on your feet! he's calling you." throwing his cloak aside, he jumped to his feet and came to jesus.

"what do you want me to do for you?" jesus asked him.

the blind man said, "rabbi, i want to see."

"go," said jesus, "your faith has healed you." immediately he received his sight and followed jesus along the road.

mark 10:46-52

my haven was under the bed.

it was a canopy-four-poster extravagantly sized queen with an immense space underneath, just waiting for someone like me to claim it.

i made it my safe place, my home, and draped an old yellow blanket around the bottom to shelter me from prying eyes. i spent hours there, secreted away, reading. i pulled an old bendable lamp, bare-bulbed, without a shade, down into the space so my eyes wouldn't go bad, so i wouldn't have to eat more carrots, to give the words their due light.

in one moment the yellow blanket was on fire, turned into an inferno by the bare bulb too close to the fraying yellow fabric. the smell of smoke was danger, was a warning. and then the footsteps from the other room. my father bending over me, the punishment, the decree.

"you are never to go under there again. you have lost the privilege."

i stopped reading for a while.

my whole life has been an experiment in finding safety.

emotionally i dwell too close to the bare bulb, on the edge of unexpected inferno, terrified of losing my privilege.

i drape my wounds around me like a blanket. they shelter me, give me an excuse to be hardened, to choose to disbelieve. the pain, the longing, the betrayal—these are the strands of my coverings. i weave them together to create a protection that, though it is made of unsafe things, provides a safety and a haven that keeps me secure. taken together, in their collective woundedness, they are strong.

i like them that way.

a god who wants my woundedness but not my covering—

what kind of god is that?

a shivering god, a jealous god. "give me yourself," he says, "trust me without these protections, trust me with your pure vulnerabilities."

and i laugh.

"and what will you do with them?" i wonder, knowing all too well what this means.

the rage wells up within me, like fire.

"and what have you done? what have you saved me from? i have spent a lifetime yearning for you, aching, longing, desiring to be whole more than any other thing. i have brought as much as i could to your feet—passed them over, surrendered my will, and all i have received is silence. this much i have given, and would give more, but for a word, an acknowledgement, a sense of comfort. and yet there is still nothing.

"you ask me to be vulnerable, and i have been. you ask me to surrender, and i stand before you already empty-handed. you ask for my trust, and yet you have never earned it. how can i dare to believe you are good if my life has been filled with so much bad done in your name, if you cannot even respond to all that i have already sought, to answer that which i have already asked? i cannot trust what is untrustworthy."

the anger fills me up with a sticky blackness, a tangible sludge inside me.

i am so angry. i have been so angry for so many years, yet i walk a fine balance between anger and fear. which feels safer? which will get me through? often i fear the anger itself, the way it rises up in me, clutching and desperate and needy.

to please the church i have squashed my anger down, squelched its desperate need, made it pretty, turned it into a rabid sense of social justice and a hatred of evil. i have made my anger acceptable, given it the definition it needs to be justified, to be righteous.

the church tells me not to be angry. it says that my anger is a sin.

in the christian world i grew up in, denying your anger was part of accepting that god was in control, that you trusted in him completely. anger had no place because there was never any right to feel like you owned any part of your life. anger reflected a sense of control, a sense of entitlement.

good christians didn't get angry. good christians believed anger meant you didn't trust god.

but god said to jonah, "do you do well to be angry for the plant?"
and he said, "i do well to be angry, angry enough to die."

jonah 4:9-10

these hands clenched: through prayer or anger, or both.

even as the words fall from my fingers, even as the sentences form on the tips of my hands, i struggle.

i am fighting with my own soul.

i long for him.

this savior, so long held up, so long adored. this jesus, so revered, so perfectly blameless. he is intertwined into my very being, incorporated into my very sense of life. he is, i believe, the fulfillment of all i ache for, the completion of all in me that is broken.

flicker: this light, an ember, a small miracle along the path.

i lay beneath my father's body and prayed.

they weren't holy prayers—prayers of devotion or faithfulness or praise—they were prayers for help, cries for deliverance. they were raw and ragged, full of despair and pain and betrayal and brokenness.

my father sometimes forced my eyes open, made me look at him as he raped me. i live with the visions of his face still. sometimes from the depths of the middle of the night i wake up screaming. sometimes i pray, and my father's face is the face of the god i see in my mind. his face comes to me in the middle of church, as i'm driving down the road, i see him in the soap bubbles in the sink. out of nowhere i see his eyes behind the eyes of a friend.

sometimes my prayers were from the part of me that disappeared. as my father raped me, i would leave my body and escape his brutality. i hid in the ceiling, i took refuge just outside my window, i found a quiet place in the back of my mind that he couldn't reach.

but he always reached me in the end. he threatened me, he teased me, he blamed me. he took everything that i believed about the world, everything that hid inside of me—the precious parts of who i was—and twisted and violated them. he broke me. he took my personhood and shattered it. he took my innocence and smashed it. he took the god i wanted to believe in and made him an animal.

i believed it was my fault, that i asked for it, that i wanted it. i believed i seduced my father, that he was confused, that when my mother left he simply replaced her with me. i had her name, i was a female, i was an easy substitute. i still believe it.

perhaps there is some part of me that wants that illusion

of power. perhaps there is some part of me that needs to believe it was my mother's fault, that she made him do it so i could have some kind of control, some kind of choice.

i hate what my father's power has done to me. i hate that i wake up gasping for breath, that i feel his hands, his weight; that i see my body as my enemy. i hate that every moment with god is a struggle with trust. a constant questioning, a tug of war.

"please come hold me, god," i whisper. but just as he nears, i tremble and push him away. "please help me, god," i cry. but just as he reaches down, i run from his touch.

i want this god, but i don't want this god.
god has my father's face. god has my father's hands.

i am afraid of open hands. closed hands, too. hands have not been my friends; they have pushed, they have taken, they have held on.

i have always struggled with the bible phrase "seek and ye shall find" because it was always offered as something immediate; it was always a promise thrown out with the promise of instant results. the great plan of those around me: step 1, step 2, step 3.

they didn't really believe in seeking, they believed in formulas. seek—find. ask—receive. knock—door opened. end of story.

i have been seeking my entire life—for a mother who loves me, for a father who loves me, for a feeling that i matter, for validation, for community, for hope, for god.

i have been told that i must not be seeking hard enough.

tell me: are these cuts, this desperation, these pills, this rape, not hard enough?

if there is anything i believe, anything that i really believe, it's that my seeking is the only part that truly connects me to any kind of hope. it is the hope in the eventuality of finding—whenever that is—that keeps me believing, that keeps me crying out for something bigger than me, to something bigger than me, with tears that have no words.

when i was 19 i went to new england believing i could make my mother love me.

i thought if i could make her love me, i would find my redemption. she would come back, she would wrap her arms around me and fix me and make me whole again. in her arms, i would finally be good enough, i would find myself cleansed. she was the missing piece in my life—not my father with his hot heavy body and his lust and his thirst for blood—but her, with her tenderness, her soft places, those arms that had held me close to her in the tide pools, out there where no one could reach us.

i remembered that love, or what i thought was that love, but it was mingled with what i believed was her revulsion for me. if only i could convince her that i had changed, i would be accepted. i was doing everything my father wanted; i had become everything he asked for. was that good enough, in the end, for her devotion?

i had to see her to know. i had to redeem us both. us all.

i took a greyhound bus without telling anyone on the east coast i was coming. i washed my hair in bus station sinks, hugged my stuffed animal in the back seat through the midwest, and wore my hard contact lenses six days straight.

i arrived exhausted, dirty, and full of expectation. my mother would love me, she would be there for me. then i would know i had found my salvation, and she, too, would forgive me; my world would be complete.

but my mother wasn't there for me;
she was hardly there for herself. she was homeless and addicted and loud and inappropriate. she was constantly

being thrown in jail for public drunkenness. she had her own vision of her own life and what she thought of me (when she thought of me at all). i only existed as part of her fantasy family, an imaginary circle of love, the pictures of crows she cut out of magazines and taped to her notebooks. "we are all crows," she told her friend cindi, "my children and i."

the mother i had hoped for was gone.

i got an apartment and a job with an environmental organization, and i started to build a life of my own. as i walked to work in the mornings, sometimes i'd see my mother sprawled on a bench in a downtown park. sometimes i would start to approach her, but my fear of her, my fear of what she thought of me, the disappointment of her lack of love, turned me away.

instead i fell in love with the lesbian couple next door to me—they gave me everything my mother could not. love and acceptance radiated from them. i ate dinner with them nearly every night, vegetarian concoctions with spices and tofu, poppy seed dressing made from scratch, artichoke stalk spaghetti, and i finally felt something close to being satisfied. something close to home.

they helped me believe that there was nothing shameful about being a woman. they helped me learn to love myself, in little bits, in little moments, and through their acceptance and their joyous countenances, i felt a wounded part of me begin to heal.

one afternoon i was painting in my apartment when there was a knock on my door.

thinking it was my friends, i opened it recklessly, and was shocked to see my mother standing there.

how had she found me? what did she want?

she was drunk, nearly incoherent, and she wrapped her arms around me, clinging to me in desperation. i tried to push her away. she stank of week-old liquor and bad weed, but she gripped harder.

"please let me live with you," she said. "i need a place to live. and i want to bring jamie, too."

she released her hold on me, stepped back, turned her head, and an 18-year-old kid, her lover, entered the room. he looked as bad as she did, but he was much younger. he stood looking at me, and i felt myself start to tremble. i was afraid of him. i was afraid of her. i was afraid of losing my frail beginnings of wholeness.

i took a deep breath. "no," i said quietly. "no, i can't let you live here. there isn't enough room."

and there wasn't enough room. but i was a coward. i was ashamed. i was more afraid of her, of him, than i was crowded. i was afraid of being taken advantage of, afraid of her rejection, afraid that she would hurt me by her presence, by her disapproval. i was afraid that the part of me that had started to feel love would be trampled on, beaten back down into nothingness.

"no," i said again. "i'm sorry."

rage filled my mother's face. she started flailing her arms at me, trying to hit me. curses flew out of her mouth, insults. she called me selfish and lazy and arrogant. she called me my father's whore. i stood there, not moving, not breathing,

waiting for her to finish, and only after she'd stomped out
of my apartment and slammed the door did i allow myself
to cry.

a few days later, flooded with desperation and grief and
guilt, i tried to kill myself. i took an overdose—six bottles
of sleeping pills and three bottles of aspirin. the doors were
locked, but somehow the couple from next door got inside
and pulled me across the floor between our apartments,
forcing me over the toilet. "throw up," they said. "we want
you to live."

nobody had ever wanted me to live before.

in the hospital they pumped my stomach, and i was angry.
faces appeared over my bed. doctors, psychiatrists, an angry
uncle. "why did you try to do this?" they all asked. i turned
my face away and didn't answer. i didn't have the words.

once they knew i would live, they dumped me into the acute
psychiatric intensive care unit the next day, and my friends
from next door came to visit, smelling of sandalwood,
bringing me flowers and friendship bracelets and dried
leaves.

"we're sorry to tell you this now, but we're moving," they
said. "we've been planning it for awhile, but we wanted to
surprise you. please come with us. we'll wait for you to get
out of here, and then we'll all go together. won't you come
with us?"

i looked into their eyes, into their faces, and echoes of my
words to my mother filled my head. i knew in that moment
that if i went, i had no chance for redemption. i would have
been happy, i would have believed in myself, and i would
have known love, but i would not have been redeemed. i
would not really have found peace.

all that they offered me, the love and kindness and
friendship, was only the beginning of me becoming whole.
it was only a birth to my healing, not the completion of it.
if i had gone with them, i would never have really found
myself, never really found the wounded broken part of me.
i would have simply used someone else to cover who i had
been. i would have let them recreate me into who i had
always wanted to believe i was rather than do the hard work
of changing who i had always been. i would never have truly
healed.

i had to say no.

they drove away on a sunny-but-chilly afternoon in their
beat-up car with the indigo girls playing loudly. i stood on
the sidewalk and waved long after they had disappeared
from my sight.

for months after they left i snuck into their empty
apartment and lay on the floor. i opened the windows to the
night sky and stared up into the stars, imagining all i had
lost, all i had believed in, all that i had wanted for my life.

my mother became physically unavailable but remained
emotionally significant, a blurry entity who always lurked
in the back of my mind, a woman who breathed with my
breath and spoke with my words. and still, everything i did,
everything i became, was an attempt to make up for the loss
of her. everything i lived was an attempt to fill in the space
she left behind.

i was one of my mother's crows.

i am still flying over the carcass of my
childhood, looking for remnants to nibble on.

i see now
there was so much i wanted
that i reached for it all and my heart broke
in the reaching, as my arms extended,
i found myself unable to defend myself.

they touched the parts i
could not protect.

oh god
why did you choose to use
people
why did you make us so
vulnerable

why do you let others
stand in your shapes
speak as in your voice
why do they have that power?

i have always posed a lot of questions that made a lot of people in the church uncomfortable. to many of those people my questions were insignificant, and their responses were hastily muttered under their breath. i don't think they ever even really thought about anything i said. they didn't want to confront their own questions, their own doubts, and they labeled me dangerous. i was considered a troublemaker.

this made it difficult to ever be taken seriously. i was silenced before i ever found the courage to speak. i was told half-truths before the questions ever left my lips.

slowly i began to see that their problem wasn't with me or with my questions as much as it was with the inevitable (but never verbalized) answer: "i don't know."

it was imperative that they "know"—even if that meant age-old platitudes grown hollow and insignificant through years of recitation. it was important that they ease concern and fears, that they comfort troubled hearts, that they clutch tightly to their faith. and the best way to accomplish that was to shut down all wondering insecurities, to shut down all doubts and disbelieving thoughts, including their own.

i heard a lot of the same things:

"god always provides."

"god will not give you anything you can't handle."

"god will make a way for escape."

these pat answers were thrown back at me as weapons, as ways to silence my questions. but while these kinds of statements were usually sucked right from the pages of scripture, and therefore bore some element of truth, they became meaningless to me with their overuse. they became weak and powerless in the face of real wondering and truthful searching.

but even more, they were pat answers to those who offered them. they were easy explanations, cut-and-pasted christian phrases guaranteed to stifle honest exploration into pain and turn god into a magic 8 ball with answers that fit any situation.

the truth in them was stripped out; the whole story in them was eliminated: god doesn't always provide when we think he should, and sometimes, his provision looks nothing like what we expect it to. god may not give more than we can handle, but it doesn't mean that we don't hurt under the weight of what he has already given us. god might provide a way of escape, but it might begin past the path of grief or sorrow or betrayal.

in my journey toward god, one of the greatest things i have learned is that there is much i do not know. sometimes that really ticks me off. why is it that i don't know what's going on here? why isn't there some kind of answer for me? what kind of god lives in these "i don't knows"? what kind of god keeps such secrets?

if there's anything i've learned about not knowing, it's that it reveals the depth of my trust. can i trust a god who will not explain himself? can i trust a god who leaves me not knowing his purpose, his will? can i trust something beyond the pat answers, the snatched promises, the ways we quiet ourselves when the questioning grows too strong?

can i trust a god who lets me live with an "i don't know" and expects that it is enough?

when i was a child, there was a major airline crash in our quiet community. my father took me to see the wreckage. we stood in the middle of the charred, desolate area—among the burned houses and the airplane ruins, fear and death all around us—and he told me stories about revenge and god's omniscience and punishment.

wandering around, my eyes open for proof, i scoured the remains for leftover remnants of the judgment of the almighty, and i blinked when i saw it—a large dirty puddle with something hiding in it, something peering up through the water at me.

my father saw me staring at it, walked over to the puddle, and picked the object up.

"it's an eye," he said. "it's the all-seeing eye of god, ripped out of a human's body and made holy through the fire of purification."

i was speechless as he quickly flashed it in my direction, then put it in his pocket.

they are all mixed together in my head: god's wrath, airplane crashes and other major disasters, body parts, good and bad, sin and sanctification, holy punishment and the fires of hell.

sometimes i am still that nine-year-old girl standing in that field; standing among the houses towering over the crash's war zone; the houses still intact screaming of second chances and lucky breaks. sometimes i'm still that nine-year-old girl who was convinced that her death for her own mistakes was ever-present and imminent. sometimes i recognize underlying lava flowing through me—a glowing red sticky substance that threatens to take away everything i love, everything i hold onto as treasure.

i struggle to be brave in these moments of doubt, of fear. i struggle to believe in the goodness of some people, in a hope for the world. i want to believe that i can go on, that i will overcome the remembering, that some day the things in my head will separate, and i will be whole.

the all-seeing eye of god watches me still. it stares at me in my memory, burning a hole in the pocket of my father's pants.

i feel an ongoing fury at the comparison of god with father. i swallow tears every time, every single time, someone prays to our "heavenly father," "father in heaven," or any variation thereof.

i have tried to change it. i have tried to close my ears, hum to myself, tell my brain that they don't mean it; they don't mean *that* father—*my* father. but the reality stays. as they say those words the anger and grief well up in me, and i feel everything clench, everything tighten, everything close off. the frightened parts of me prepare for the pain, for the disapproval, and i sit there hunched over quietly, feeling small and scared.

how can you dare to compare yourself to a father, god? who are you to think that i can ever trust you with that perception? who are you to give me that image and then give me my father? why did you give an example that went so badly? why did you insist on a relationship that was so wrong?

what chance do i have of knowing you apart from him, apart from his influence on me?

what chance did i ever have?

in my mind
i am standing on the edge
jagged rocks
steep cliff
river snaking through the reddened clay.

in my mind
you took away escape
freedom's bridge
safety's harness

clay hugging the winding river
not wet enough
not pure enough
to wash myself of these stains.

in my mind
you took my childhood
my hope
my sense of security
and blamed him
for everything you were and had done.

every single sunday, at the end of every single service, the pastor gave an invitation.

the church swelled with the sounds of people in praise, extended verses of "just as i am" echoed throughout the room, and my father stood next to me, elbowing me in the side.

"go," he whispered under his breath. "go."

i laughed, knowing he was just trying to bother me, just trying to make me uncomfortable, but i prayed the prayer under my breath anyway, just to be sure, drowning in a doubt i couldn't name.

the years passed, and i kept accepting jesus—at summer camp, brokenhearted over my motherlessness; moments before a band competition, because i wanted us to win; under my breath in the shower, driving down the street, at the end of a chapel service—i prayed the magic prayer of salvation any time i needed a hit of jesus, a feel-good dime bag of christianity.

the high lasted until the depression returned. and then the insecurity swirled in again—choking me with its intensity. my worthlessness, my inability to believe bubbled inside me until i was foaming at the mouth with it, and finally, in desperation, i raised my fist and screamed out my pain, but the heavens were silent.

pastors chimed in—dozens of them. at spiritual emphasis week, at senior retreat: i wasn't praying hard enough, i wasn't reading my bible enough. "get perspective, focus on others," they said. so i spent hours praying for those with less, for the persecuted christians around the world, for

those truly suffering for their faith. and at the last amen i
still only felt sadness for their situations and a bitter jealousy
that they had a faith that was worth giving their lives for.

the packaged prayer was always on my lips: i breathed
jesus into my heart over and over and over, never feeling
loved, never feeling good enough, always feeling my father
standing next to me, his elbow piercing my side, invisible
bruises on my very soul.

"go," the words echo inside of me, "go."

dear lord jesus, four spiritual laws, god-shaped vacuum, the bridge across the chasm, come into my heart, take away my sin, fill me with your holy spirit—but oh god you have no idea how bad i am, how dirty, how much i have done. how could you want me? how could someone like me be worth your redemption?

and what if i don't want you? what if i don't trust you?
what if i'm furious that after all these years, all these prayers,
i haven't felt any lasting connection, any certainty? what
privacy can i have left if i invite you in?

my father took whatever he wanted from me. my body was
his. and my soul was his, too. he created me in his image,
he defiled me even in your name. and you allowed it. you
allowed him to use your name to defile me.

what if i can't bear the thought of you?

i sit in church, trembling, and i hear my father's voice, and i
make it my own.

"go," i say to the jesus who stands once again at my heart and waits patiently for me to open the door and sup with him (and he with me). "i don't trust you. i am afraid of you. i have let you in a thousand times and nothing has changed."

———

in my mind
i am standing on the edge
jagged rocks
steep cliff
river snaking through the reddened clay.

glancing down
i see images of my past
my father's face in the crevices,
shame in the fast-running water,
blood screaming out from the ground.

in my mind
i want to feel brave
and confident and free
but i only feel despair
and longing
and fear.

when i found out that i was pregnant, i was going to an episcopal church. it wasn't the episcopal church that began my path to healing, though; it was an episcopal church in drag. disguised as different, it was as conservative as the baptist church i grew up in.

the priest seemed like a wonderful man— until i talked about my struggles with having the baby. he assumed i would have it, that i would do the right thing. it was not open for negotiation. it was not even a choice.

when i called him, in tears, from the pay phone by the sanctuary of my christian college, he told me that if i had an abortion he would call my father and tell him.

"but i told you under the rite of confession," i said. "you can't do that."

"it doesn't matter," he said. "i am willing to give up the secrecy and sanctity of confession for life."

and i wonder, still, even now: what about my life?

i was terrified at the priest's words. i felt broken and isolated. i felt betrayed. i felt like i couldn't even express how fearful i was. i couldn't express my terror, my confusion, any doubts. i couldn't express anything.

so i ran to the east coast to have an abortion. and when i did, and when the truth came out to the priest, he refused to speak to me ever again. he handed the phone to his wife, and he told her to tell me that i was dead to him. that i had better find another priest and confess the sin of murder. that he would never ever love me again. he said that his love had been falsely invested.

and some part of me, all these years later, has never forgiven myself for what i did.

i disappointed god. i didn't have enough faith.

i committed murder, i cared more for myself than for a child, and i was not brave.

dear god,
giver of life,
i am a life-taker.
i am one who has crushed that which you have created
because i was afraid, because i was alone,
because i took that life (and mine)
into my own hands.

what do i want from you,
here in this moment,
in this empty space,
what would satisfy my soul?

there is such pain in me.
it feels bottomless.
there is such sadness,
it seizes me and it paralyzes me
and i can't think past it.

such rage lurking under my skin,
questions, fears,
everything bad i buried
deep inside my soul
trying desperately
to be good.

i feel such unbelievable emptiness.

it feels like the innermost part of me was sucked out; like i have purged myself of all of my futilities and am discovering in the end that i am only a hollow chasm of nothing.

when the pain is there, it fills me up; it makes me collapse with weak aching. i split down the middle with the agony of it.

i wonder if my father could see me now...would he laugh? would he repent? would he simply not care?

i wonder who i am underneath this emptiness. i wonder if i can ever find the innocence i had before the fall: before incest, before the initial death of my soul.

and perhaps it is a deadening that i am feeling. a calloused roughening over what used to pulsate, to thrive, to live loudly—perhaps it is a sadness mixed with shame that is so terrible and so deep that it can't be defined.

i am burned out on evangelism, on god in tiny boxes. i am tired of designating things as christian or secular, tired of wearing these old tattered spiritual clothes that pass for kingly garments.

here's a secret: the emperor is naked.

we must redefine what we mean by "evangelism." we must redefine what we mean by "believer." we must consider connection, storytelling, engagement, and reflection as necessary for our spirituality. we must become more human, more aware of who we are, of who god is, of all that lingers within us, hiding underneath our unholy rags.

i am weary, tired, exhausted, and worn out. the pretending is bigger than i am. i want to be real. i want to have real conversations, hear real stories, share real thoughts.

the four spiritual laws are not the gospel. "amazing grace" and swaying choirs are not the gospel.

the gospel is who.

the gospel is why.

the gospel is, "lord i believe, help thou my unbelief."

i do.

oh jesus, help me, for i do not.

"i want you to pick a topic that you personally struggle with," the professor said as he handed out a list of topics. "i want this to be more than just a report and a discussion. i want this to be a process for you."

i skimmed the list and immediately settled on a basic question: the existence of god.

i had never dared to admit that i doubted the existence of god before, but it was something that i struggled with—not because i genuinely wondered if he was there, but because i had chosen not to believe in him.

i decided that it was safer to not believe in him at all than it was to believe in him and then hate him or be angry with him.

everything in my life told me that god cannot handle my emotions, and so i shut him down. i closed myself off to him entirely rather than be real.

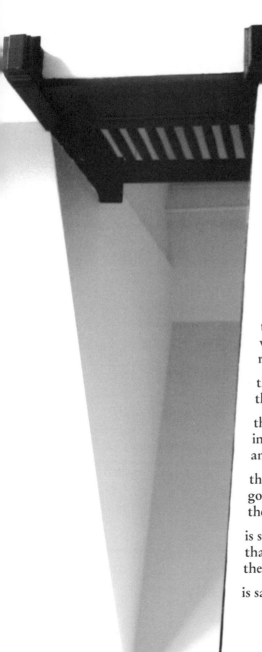

"i am angry"
"i hurt"
"where are you, god?"

these words
require

trust
vulnerability
risk

the space to be honest
the space to be genuine

the space to be
in pain
and still believe

that the
god you ask
these questions of

is still there
that the god you ask
these questions of

is safe.

my father stood in front of my third-grade class explaining his job. he talked about germs and how he helped make places for germs to grow.

it was a simplistic explanation, one i'd heard countless times.

he passed out a petri dish to each person in the class, told us to cough several times on them, and then write our names in magic markers on tape on the top lid. after we did this, he collected them and handed them to our teacher, who placed them in her empty desk drawer and locked it.

we weren't allowed to look at them while they cultivated.

a week later, my father returned to our classroom and, with dramatic flourish and high anticipation, removed the petri dishes from the teacher's desk drawer and set them on her desk.

the students clustered around, curious to see what they had produced.

within minutes, one particular petri dish stood out. it was covered with spores, with germs. they were stacked on top of each other.

the other children looked at it with disgust and slowly backed away. then there were collective giggles and some of the girls whispered to each other behind their hands.

i realized, as my knees trembled beneath me, that the petri dish was mine.

i found out about my mother's death on the internet.

i had typed her name into google hundreds of times before and came up empty. but this time, there were links.

she died homeless in the snow.

i stopped breathing for a few minutes.

and then there were only tears.

she carried me close to her, a handkerchief on her head, flowers tucked behind her ears. smelling of patchouli and pot, she made the beach circuit—stopping for some good music, some good conversation, some good weed—until finally we arrived at the tide pools. she let me explore, on hands and knees; she pointed out the creatures that spit brilliant pink and purple ink; she gave me the unbroken sand dollars. i sat between her legs, leaning against her frail frame and felt the water rush in, watching the crabs swirl around our toes, tasting the salt on my lips. nobody could touch us out on the rocks. we were invincible, independent; only the water, which we embraced, could flood in.

a snapshot in my mind, the feeling of her behind me, the wind flinging my hair, the salt on my lips, the ocean rushing to us, the whitewater breaking nearby, the exhilaration. my mom, my mother—this woman i only know through the feel of my own body, my own struggles with addictions, with bottomless emptiness, with need—she gave me a love for the ocean, the safety of it, the sanctuary of it.

for so long i've had a hope that i've been afraid to think about or acknowledge. it was the hope of somehow finding a family again—my family. my mother would be saved. she would find me, and we would reconcile, and we would love each other without dilution, and all of the awfulness of my life would be somehow okay. just because of her. because of us.

in the back of my head, all these years, she was my only hope. she was the one who could fix everything, who could make me okay again. if she would—if she could—only come back again, i'd know i was forgivable. i'd know i could be loved.

and now she's gone. gone. my hopes, my wishes, everything that was part of my fantasy storybook ending—gone. my hope of redemption as someone worthy of love—gone. my friend, my source, the only one who knew what it was really like to live with my father—gone.

she wasn't in my life, but she was a foundation for my life. so much of who i am is built on top of the reality of her. so many of my feelings, my fears, my desires are dependent on her being alive, on her being on the same planet, breathing the same air, looking at the same stars.

my mother was as much a part of my life as if she'd been in it every day. she was a part of who i am, of how i look at myself, of how i function in the world. she was the hidden part of me that wanted to believe that my life wasn't what it was, that i had a secret, an escape. a mother who hadn't yet come back because i hadn't proven to her that i was worthy of it.

my whole life has been a struggle to prove to her that she should love me.

but she's gone, and now there's a gaping blackness in me that's bigger than anything else inside me.

it is deep and dark. and it is bottomless.

oh mom. oh mom. i ache for you. i have always ached for you.

oh god,
can you please be my mother for me?
can you please love me where she couldn't,
forgive me where she didn't,
hold me like i always wanted her to?
if i can believe that you are safe,
can you shelter me from this relentless longing,
this indescribable pain?

i have always been afraid of my sadness.

i have learned to smother it, to hide it from the world, from the light, from my consciousness. christians are supposed to be happy. we are allowed our moments of grief, but after a designated time, we are supposed to move on. the gratitude of salvation, the joy of being forgiven—they ultimately give us hope, make us okay again. we're supposed to believe that nothing can separate us from the love of god and not admit those times we feel unloved and separated.

"don't forget, we have the victory! we have won the war!" the church said to me. "it's just this battle that feels so dark and hard and frustrating."

the church used bible verses to defend this point of view. yanked verbatim from the pages of the king james bible, they were quoted and re-quoted and ultimately turned into weapons.

"all things work together for good."

"be anxious for nothing."

sadness meant lack of faith. unbelief. there was a point at which sadness intertwined with sin, and that's when others shut down, refused to hear me, assigned it as a problem needing forgiveness.

there is a part of me that is in continual pain. sometimes i walk through a crowd of people barely able to keep my composure. i still cry myself to sleep. my sadness is sometimes bottomless; it won't let me meet my own eyes in the mirror.

when jesus saw her weeping,
and the jews who had come
along with her also weeping, he
was deeply moved in spirit and
troubled...

jesus wept.

john 11:33,35

i spent some time in a pentecostal church.

i didn't ever flop down and roll with holiness, but i did my share of out-of-control shaking and incoherent mumbling.

the seeds for charismatic behavior were planted during my years attending an assembly of god elementary school. i went to 6th grade camp and came home speaking in tongues. my father was a noncharismatic, untongued baptist and was completely beside himself. he made me call a local christian radio show to talk this over with the host who spent a half hour on live radio trying to convince me that tongues weren't a spiritual gift anymore. after this failed to get through to me (i had an experience to argue my point, after all), i spent hours sitting at the kitchen table with my father, a collection of conservative books stacked next to a big black king james bible open to 1 corinthians 14.

my father's biggest competition in his attempt to correct me was my very charismatic elementary school. they fully believed in the gifts of the spirit, including the controversial gifts of tongues and prophecy, and their beliefs directly conflicted with all the beliefs my father was trying so desperately to instill in me. i went to bible class and heard them talk about the baptism of the spirit, the gift of prophecy, and then came home to the opposite opinion.

it all ended when my father was skimming my 8th grade yearbook and found an admonition from my best friend: "remember to speak in tongues over the summer."

unable to convert me and now assured that even my friends were trapped in the charismatic lie, my father sent me to a noncharismatic, baptist high school and college for the rest of my education.

many years later, and at a particularly empty period in my life, i wandered into a pentecostal church. i sat down, looked around, and felt something kind of like home.

the women had long hair; some of them had never cut it. they wore skirts instead of pants, and they wore no jewelry at all—not even wedding rings. they had a lot of verses to support their sparseness, and they seemed to take some pride at being different from the rest of the world. but what repeatedly affected me was their passion.

these were some of the most passionate people i had ever met.

i remember them standing in a darkened room, waiting for the spirit of god, seeking some invisible jolt of spiritual electricity—and when it fell upon them, they rocked and cried and wailed. they allowed their emotional experiences to reflect their spiritual experiences; they were of the opinion that emotions were part of god's working power—it was a welcomed contrast to a life of being told that the spiritual facts should override the human feelings.

that emotional connection with god never came to me in those later years at the pentecostal church. i had been thoroughly convinced by then that spirit and emotion were separate realms, and that my emotions were sinful. i tried to reach it as i had in 6th grade, but i never again experienced that visible display of passion. i only felt tired and sore and embarrassed at the end of the night, and as much as i babbled my tongue, pushed my hands skyward and sobbed, i was never filled or satisfied.

i saw the statue of mary standing in the flower garden and was drawn to her. i admired her face, the lifelike flowing of her clothes, and felt compelled to wait with her awhile.

i looked into her eyes. they were hollow and dead, and the more i looked, the more disturbed i was. what was i seeking in this statue, this silent witness to my pain? what was she trying to show me?

after a time i noticed her hands. they were badly maintained, many of the fingers broken off at the knuckles. her left thumb was coming apart, bits of the wire underneath peeking through—it was a stark and unexpected color in contrast to her polished whiteness.

and then i realized what i needed to know.

these are my hands.

broken and damaged, i try, i long, to hold them out. i want to experience risk, to accept good things, to be okay. i reach for that which i know will satisfy. i stretch my arms for that which will give me validation.

but my fingers are broken off. the fear and sadness peek through my best attempts at courage. the love i seek, the love i want to hold, falls right through.

holiness lives somewhere in me, a creature curled up, waiting simply to be noticed.

there is an invisible barrier between who i am and who i am supposed to become.

after years of being defined by others, their messages echoing in my head, i am convinced of who they say they see. it is a reality etching itself into my own skin late at night, in the bathroom, in the dark. i rock back and forth and weep.

woe is me, for i am undone.

i try to grasp hold of myself, who i am, and the definition slips through my fingers.

my mother has died, and with her death a shell peeled around me, only to be replaced by thicker, more intense protection. perhaps i realize how alone i really am in this world without her; how much bigger the planet is; how far away the stars are. perhaps i realize, on some unspoken but very real level, i could have done more, should have done more. the guilt wraps around me like a burial shroud.

today, two different people at different times looked at me as if they could see the pain i keep so carefully tucked underneath. their eyes softened as they looked in mine. i looked away instantly but felt a twinge in the deep places where my sadness hides.

there is a constant emotional investment in appearing composed, as composed as is possible for me. it's exhausting simply keeping my face from melting, my eyes from tearing up, my lungs from screaming: help me, o god help me, help me o god.

and what it comes down to in the end is that i need help, but i have no idea what i need, nor do i know what would actually help. i feel numb and dead most of the time, full of broken shattered stuff; hollow, as if i make no difference in the world.

the decoration on top, what others see, is merely overcompensation, pretending, utilizing every ounce of strength i have to make it through the day.

i want my mother back. i want my mother back, and i want to fly across the country and hug her and hold her. i want to believe that I can go on without her, that somehow part of her is still here. i want tide pools and patchouli and sand dollars.

i want to believe that i am good.

now thomas (called didymus), one of the twelve, was not with the disciples when jesus came. so the other disciples told him, "we have seen the lord!"

but he said to them, "unless I see the nail marks in his hands and put my finger where the nails were, and put my hand into his side, i will not believe it."

a week later his disciples were in the house again, and thomas was with them. though the doors were locked, jesus came and stood among them and said, "peace be with you!" then he said to thomas, "put your finger here; see my hands. reach out your hand and put it into my side. stop doubting and believe."

thomas said to him, "my lord and my god!"

then jesus told him, "because you have seen me, you have believed; blessed are those who have not seen and yet have believed."

john 20:24-29

i have heard this passage so often. it has been used to explain to modern-day christians how blessed we are, how brave we are—for believing without sight.

i have heard pastors mock thomas for his disbelief. i have heard thomas used as an example of what not to be, of someone to aspire above.

by not going to church have i, too, missed jesus' coming? where was thomas that he wasn't with the others? where am i? what am i missing by being away?

perhaps i don't want to see jesus, to see his glory, his presence. perhaps i stay away to avoid him.

i know i don't want to see the version of jesus i've grown up with—the one who considers me unworthy, the one who cannot hear my pain. i lock the doors, i wear the cloak, and yet underneath i still feel this yearning, this longing, a hungering hiding in me that is beyond description.

is he the kind of jesus who comes when the doors are locked? do i want that kind of jesus? how can i respect one who does not respect locks?

i grew up with the bible—i tucked it under my pillow at night and stuffed it into my backpack with my battered binder and christian textbooks during the day. we memorized verses at my christian school, in second-period bible class, in each of my assorted church activities, and my father had a repetition he required at bedtime.

my whole life was an exploration in literalism—everybody around me, in my church's religious and denominational circles, everybody in my connection with religion, believed that the bible was the definite, infallible (*inerrant* was thrown around a lot) word of god. everybody was certain that every jot, every tittle (a word that continually made us junior highers roll on the carpet in prepubescent laughter) was inspired and absolutely not debatable.

there were no other options, no other interpretations, no hint of social or cultural context. what had been written was engraved in stone, was unchangeable, as literal as the morning sun and the promise of eventual rain.

in many ways, this kind of thinking, this literalism, set me up.

as an abused child with very little redemption in my life, the more i saw a god who was literal in his judgments, the more his wrath alienated me from the concept of god altogether.

what was the difference between this man who called himself my father and this heavenly father who seemed to approve so much of the earthly one?

in my current pursuit of god, i find myself crawling from underneath literalism. at least i am trying. for even as i reach toward something that just might be poetic or symbolic, i feel the fires of hell breathing on my backside; i feel something in me cry "heretic, heretic, burn her!" i feel one misplaced mark of punctuation dooming me to an eternity in torment.

now brothers, about times and dates we do not need to write to you, for you know very well that the day of the lord will come like a thief in the night. while people are saying, "peace and safety," destruction will come on them suddenly, as labor pains on a pregnant woman, and they will not escape.

1 thessalonians 5:1-3

black helicopters still scare me.

i was in my formative years during the first wave of apocalypse fever.

through *the late great planet earth* and *a thief in the night* (the movie series), i quickly came to understand that my life was fleeting, that nothing was permanent, and that i had to live my life constantly knowing the end could come at any time.

a thief in the night terrified me. i had apocalyptic nightmares about vans and guillotines and woke from them lying in bed afraid to move—certain i was the only one in the house, that i had been left behind.

it isn't exaggerating to say i was traumatized by the constant bombardment of the threat of the end of the world. whether it was specific to (or worsened by) my father, whether it was a side effect of the time period and denomination i grew up in, or whether it was all of the above, i still do not know.

i know only that all these years later i still freeze in terror at the sound of helicopters. all these years later i battle minute by minute feeling unworthy, second by second feeling not good enough or holy enough—all these years later i still live with a black gnawing hole in the pit of my stomach, filling me with dread.

so many in the church assume that good intentions justify anything. they believe saving someone from hell or the tribulation or the dreaded glinting guillotine from *a thief in the night* makes any method they use—even terror— perfectly fine.

the truth was that my father didn't have good intentions. he deliberately and constantly instilled in me fear, mistrust, shame, guilt, worthlessness. and my associate pastor, my christian schools, and my church were his mistresses in that deliberate instillation—regardless of their good intentions. he provided the threats, and they provided the scenario and the repetition to make them true.

many christians talk about the security of salvation, a sense of certainty, but i don't see how i will ever have that. no matter how many times i pray the sinner's prayer or fall on my knees with the four spiritual laws on my lips, i don't believe i will ever assume that i won't be left here; that when the end of the world comes, i won't be forgotten.

in my mind's eye, i will always see the glint of that guillotine shining, waiting to chop off my head. i will always hear my father's voice, insisting that i will never be loved. i will always fear the sound of helicopters and twitch at the sight of dark vans and dams. it's ingrained in me like my blood. with my blood. in my blood.

it's part of who i am.

o god,
your love does pull at me,
if i am silent with myself
i feel it,
as much as i feel my blood, my breath,
it is there, as present with me as my own self.

it terrifies me, this love of yours.
what does it expect in return?
what will it demand of me?
what part of who i am must i sacrifice for it?
how much of me will be lost?

i am afraid of losing what i have left
so much has already been taken away
so much i never gave,
so much i was never able to give
because it was never really mine.

i am afraid that your love will take me apart
that it will undo me, rewrite me,
that it will strip me of my defenses,
my pathetic self-securities,
that it will leave nothing left.

my whole life has been a fear of being nothing.
i have held onto my terror, my shame, my grief,
believing it helped to keep me alive.

what does your love do with my shame?
what does your love do with everything in me that
resists it?

and always, the same questions:
where were you in those harsh times? where was
your love?

this struggle is difficult, and i am tired. sometimes salvation stands in front of me with her arms open wide, her embrace outstretched, and i am tempted. there are times when i want to embrace the christian bubble, the church at its worst. i want to jump in and immerse myself in unthinking, remote christianity. i don't want the difficulties of the cross, the crown of thorns, the dying daily.

i want something that makes me feel good, that defines me by its existence; i want the illusion of being satisfied. it is quite easy for me to embrace something so fully that i lose myself. i could return to church and let it swallow me up again. i could return to church and surrender completely to the busyness, to the distraction, to paint-by-numbers spirituality.

sometimes more than anything i want the nagging, the fighting, the struggling inside of me to go away. i want to run into bordered predictable conservative christianity—the kind that casts out demons and has three steps to whatever ails you. the kind that preaches sermons with alliterative points and gets slain in the spirit and runs laps around the sanctuary.

the longing in me is enough for that. with one plunge, i could completely turn off my brain, my emotions, my past, everything that makes me me, and go "home."

i know because sometimes i desperately want to believe in a kind of pat predictability. i know because sometimes i envy others living their lives with a blissful "faith." i know because sometimes just believing that i am the scum of the earth and god is all wonderful fits perfectly with what i was told my entire life—as ugly as it is, it's comfortable, it's familiar, and it relieves me of any responsibility or choice or individuality or purpose outside of god.

people often tell me how amazing it is that i am still searching, still seeking, still questioning after all this; they say it's a miracle that i haven't turned away entirely.

to be truthful, the miracle is that i haven't totally given in.

i resist because the god i am seeking, the god i am slowly finding, does not live in that christian bubble. he does not dwell among the petty scripture quotations and the "be thankful in everythings" and the pat answers that bring nothing but guilt and shame and confusion. rather he lives in every "why?" i ask, in every moment i am afraid, in every part of my heart that dares to be honest with him, in every part that even dares to question his very existence.

from childhood i was told that god was not a god of doubts. i was taught that believing the pat answers equaled independent thinking. i was taught that questioning god was sin, akin to death.

sometimes i want to believe that i shouldn't question god. i want the prescribed formula, the strict boundaries of dogmatic belief. it is safer to live under a god you can define, to know what he expects from you. it tames him. makes him manageable somehow.

the god of my childhood was small and tame and boxed in. he had no ability to be any greater than i could imagine him. he was not a god of questions; he was a god of little answers, of small things. he had no real personality.

*when he came down from the
mountainside, large crowds
followed him. a man with leprosy
came and knelt before him and
said, "lord, if you are willing, you
can make me clean."*

*jesus reached out his hand and
touched the man. "i am willing,"
he said. "be clean!" immediately he
was cured of his leprosy.*

matthew 8:1-3

i have always believed, in the deepest part of me, that i am too unclean for jesus.

i have believed that he has been unwilling to touch me, to heal me. i have believed that it has been within his power, but he has been disgusted, repulsed by who i am.

i have never asked him like the man with leprosy; i have never said, "if you are willing," because i fear the answer. i fear his response: "no, i am not willing. suffer through your uncleanliness. die in it."

there is faith in those words: "if you are willing." and there is a willingness on the leper's part, too—a willingness to be vulnerable, to risk rejection, to confront the possibility that jesus might say "no." there is a hope there as well—a hope that jesus will not turn away, that he will not be unwilling. that he will heal him.

instead i grew up with the constant caveat of the will of god.

"if it be your will, heal aunt vera. if it be your will, cure sally from cancer. if it be your will, save me."

i didn't understand why god was ever unwilling. i didn't understand why his benevolence did not sweep the whole world into his arms; why he did not simply will away disease and pain and suffering and death.

insecurities rush in fiercely—flooding my heart and my eyes. though i scream for an end to the deluge, it continues to overflow; the water continues to come.

what does it mean to stand on a lofty dry place and laugh at the torrent? what does it mean to be unaffected, to wear a lifejacket with a smirk, aware that the drowning happens even to those who can swim? what does it mean to know that in the end, we all are taken under?

i close my eyes, i flail my arms, i kick my feet—standard actions of a person who cannot relax, who cannot let go, who refuses to let the current pull her beneath the surface, down into the darkness.

but when does the darkness win?

when?

how long until the cramps come? until the overwhelming urge to surrender—gulping mouthfuls of seawater and spitting out kelp—is stronger and more powerful than i am? how long until i concede that the depths never give up? how long until the relief of effortlessness? how long until the gentle caress of my final lullaby?

then a stinging in my sinus, a searing snort, the sludge moving down the back of my throat as i recognize my fear.

i do not want to drown.

in the darkness of much of my life, there have appeared many tiny sparks of light. in the midst of being infected by poisonous people, there have always been people with good hearts trying to guide me, people who saw enough in me to acknowledge that there was pain, people who encouraged me to push forward in spite of it. although much of my relationship with christianity has been negative, and although many people joined together to dismiss much of who i was and what was going on in my life, there also have been people who were willing to separate out from the others and treat me with kindness. in my angriest, most despairing moments i know i forget about them, but they are there, and they are a part of why i am still pursuing god in any fashion, why i am still able to say that i want to believe.

as i reflect on my journey, i see that the offerings each of them gave me were only understood to the depth that i was able to accept them.

we were sitting in a church somewhere north of seattle. our choir was making a tour of churches in washington state, doing the evening services for anyone lucky enough to attend. we had a whole program put together—the choir would sing, there would be some testimonies, and our associate pastor would give the sermon.

it had been several months and several churches now, but he was still giving the same message.

several months before our choir had been on a trip to colorado. i hadn't been allowed to go—it was too close to easter. late one evening our associate pastor was driving, and he fell asleep at the wheel. the bus rolled over several times, but the only one hurt was his best friend, a great guy who volunteered to help on the trip—in fact, he was killed. his body was thrown from the bus, and he was crushed to death.

so the associate pastor made a sermon out of the tragedy—a ridiculous, meaningless cliché about falling asleep at the wheel of our christian witness. the illustration for the message was his guilt about falling asleep, the accident, his best friend's death, and the lessons he had learned about how it applied to all of us. the only things that gave the message its power were the circumstances behind it; the message itself cheapened what had actually happened.

the sermon felt hollow and numbing after a while. he preached it in our home church and on our choir tour, and we heard it service after service , the same story, the same message. the repetition stole our opportunity to grieve. it made it impossible for us to feel angry with him. after a while his best friend's death felt fabricated and meaningless.

we started thinking of him as just another sermon illustration, just another weapon used against our apathy and adolescent selfishness.

we had to have faith in god, faith in our associate pastor, faith that somehow all this had happened to guide us back to right relationships with god. we couldn't blame anyone. we had to let the associate pastor trivialize his friend's death and let it all go away in a sermon and a learned lesson and a few amy grant songs.

i became obsessed with his friend's death, with what i saw as forgotten. i became obsessed with the truth of what had happened, how frightened he must have been, how horrible the situation really had been. the bus was towed to a lot on the edge of our town, and sometimes i'd drive there, climb into it, sit in the seats, and write in my journal.

i promised myself i would never forget him. i circled every picture of him from a photocopied memory page, even those that only showed fragments of his hair or his reflection in a fast-food window. in many ways he became the representation of my despair, the proof that nobody paid attention, the denial of everything that was genuinely broken and hurting, the reality that ultimately everybody would forget.

here i am! i stand at the door and knock. if anyone hears my voice and opens the door, i will come in and eat with him, and he with me.

revelation 3:20

i've accepted jesus more times than i can count.

at a tender young age in sunday school—confronted with the bad things i had done, and certain i would face a future forever in a boiling hot hell, separated from everything and everyone i loved.

at the beginning of adolescence—6th grade camp where i was given the gift of tongues and the baptism of the holy spirit.

my junior year in high school—spiritual emphasis week and a pastor from a local church who had enough charisma and eloquence to convince me i was doomed and lost, even though i had prayed the prayer before.

twice in college—once after confronting the darkness within me and finding it terrifying; a second time when i began attending a holy roller church and felt unclean compared to the rest of the congregation.

it was the perfect blank chalkboard for me. got a father who rapes you and tells you it's your fault? accept jesus, and it will all go away. got some pain you can't define floating around inside you? accept jesus and watch all of your troubles turn to a peace that passes all understanding.

it was the holy grail for a confused, troubled teen with a zillion voices shouting around her and no quiet in which to hear her own heart.

when did i stop believing in the magic of being saved? when did the cross, the pictures of the suffering christ, become just another manipulation? why did i stop giving up on clean slates and second chances?

in a way i feel more hopeless than ever, and perhaps that has been what has constantly drawn me to the promise of redemption—a hope that somehow everything would be okay. a hope that i could be forgiven for the horrible things i had done and seen and made my daddy do to me. a hope that in the end i would find that jesus is truly a friend and a source of caring and comfort. a hope that i would no longer be alone.

yet, in the end, after every prayer, i felt more and more alone. in spite of my salvation and the holy spirit, i found myself feeling more and more depressed, wracked with anguish, and facing more pain than i had ever had before.

with forgiveness comes guilt. with salvation comes commitment. and i couldn't keep my end of the bargain. i couldn't be "perfect as your father in heaven is perfect." i couldn't "pray without ceasing" or "preach the gospel to every nation." it was all i could do to get through the day. the language of christianity and the troubles my fellow christians faced were beyond my comprehension. and my part in that whole scheme was just another part of the body of christ—one in the middle of many, as i had always been.

i wish that it was what they described. i wish i could say i've felt inexplicable peace, known the joy of forgiveness, had my life revolutionized by the cross. i want to have those moments of joy, those moments of pleasure. i want to come to the end of my life and know that it has meant something. i want that one final confirmation—i'm saved! saved! wonderfully saved, and i'm so glad i am.

but for now there's too much pain and darkness and endless doubt in my heart. for now the gospel doesn't include people who have experienced my kind of life— the pat answers or clichés mean nothing to me, and they hurt me much more than they help.

so i run to a safe place where there are no answers and clichés, no buzzwords, no lingo. and even though i am finally safe, i realize that i don't really want to be.

i want the danger, community, a chance for connection. i want a gospel that understands my kind of pain—the gospel that has room for my kind of pain. if i lock everyone out, what hands will ever offer to help lead me back home?

and where is the home i am so desperately looking for?

so much of my search for god has been a search for community, for family, for belonging, for connection.

when the mormon missionaries came to my door, young and freshly scrubbed, offering an exclusive community and the chance to belong, i wanted what they offered me. my loneliness had reached despairing levels: my cats were my best friends, and the church i was going to didn't recognize my need. i let the mormon brothers in the door, in spite of my years of bible college, my apologetics class, my 10th grade bible test on cults.

the missionaries were committed to their agenda, but they saw the longing in me, and connected me with a mormon family from the local ward. i didn't have a telephone, so the family (along with all eight children) often showed up unannounced, sometimes with food or games, and always with a lot of free time.

they filled up my studio apartment with their bodies, their laughter, their noise. they were willing to listen to me. the girls hugged me and braided my hair, and the boys fixed things around my apartment or played with my cats. they became my family; they filled the spaces inside me that wanted a mom and dad and siblings; they wrapped themselves around me with care and love and all of the things i thought i wanted and needed. they had surprisingly few expectations, and i welcomed their presence in my life.

i grew to love the family, grew to love being part of that family, and when they moved from the east coast to utah, i went with them.

i went shopping with them at the navy commissary, played games in the backyard, hung out with the women, and did crafty things. i helped to make the relief society a more creative place—filled it with words and music—and they started to ask my opinion more often.

i wanted so desperately for it to work. i wanted to belong, wanted to believe that i had a place there. but as the days and months went by, i realized how much was wrong, so much i couldn't begin to fix. i started to notice the minuscule place the women held, not only in the family, but also in the local church. the women had their own world in the church, but it was limited to that; their power was only horizontal. i saw how the men treated their wives, saw how tired and worn out the women were, started seeing the misogyny and sexism, and knew enough to understand that i was walking right back into the mentality i thought i'd run away from.

the end came one night when the father, in a political rage, slammed his fist into a desk hard enough to dent it. i had never seen him hit anyone or anything before, but in an instant all of my abuse came flooding back, and i found myself running up the stairs, out of the house and down the street. i knew the local neighbors from attending the local church, and i ran, in my flannel nightgown and bare feet, down the icy sidewalk, stopping only to pound on doors.

when one finally opened, i ran into the house, out of breath and panicky. my father's voice was echoing in my head, and i wasn't sure who i was more afraid of—the father i no longer lived with or the mormon father i had just fled from. i was confused and terrified and shaking. i curled in a ball on the neighbor's couch, with a blanket pulled over my head, feeling betrayed and lonely and desperate.

i went back to the family's home to get my things, and they didn't understand.

the children looked at me with eyes full of
questions and one of the little girls held on
to my skirt in an attempt to keep me there.
while part of me felt i was overreacting, at the
same time i knew that my reaction was valid.
i knew i was seeing glimpses of all that i had
escaped, that those feelings and fears were not
worth the feeling of family, that in the end,
the feeling of family was only an illusion if
the women weren't treated respectfully.

—

i have always been
a man-made woman.

i have always been
who they said i was
nothing more.
nothing in me
daring to ever
be more.

each tiny step
toward freedom
toward independence
has been made with
hesitancy,
with fear.

am i allowed to do this?
can i say these things?
can i walk this direction?
can i stand this way?

the deeper the vulnerability, the deeper the fear.
the more i let people into my little world, the more i am
exposed, the more danger lurks behind every face. as hidden
parts reveal, as the silence finds a voice, there are suddenly
immense and incalculable repercussions, consequences
beyond even my own understanding.

my whole life has been a quest for love.

my longing is insatiable. i have given up myself to feel love
before, to pretend to feel it. i have sold my integrity for the
fleeting illusion. i have prayed the sinner's prayer, declared
the four spiritual laws, asked jesus into my heart with fierce
desperation. love me, love me, love me, let me know.

there is a bottomless chasm in me where love falls in and
disappears. if it is given to me, pure and without agenda,
i disbelieve it. i talk it away, i cut it out of me, i make a
thousand excuses for why i am unlovable, why they really
didn't mean it. if it is a gimmick, given in order to get, it is
like my father. it feels familiar, but it doesn't fill me up, it
doesn't feel like love, like what i want, like what i really need.

there is nothing in me for love to latch on to.

there is no place for me to hold it—it falls through my
fingers, it slips through my soul, it passes right through me. i
am ashamed. i feel guilty for my disbelief, for my fear, for my
thirty thousand doubts, the lingering questions. inside me is
my father's never-ending mantra: you will never be LOVED.
you will NEVER be loved. YOU will never be loved.

is it possible to have a place where you cannot feel? is it
possible to have some part that can never believe, that can
never let go, that will always wrap her arms around herself
and protest everything she sees, everything she might feel,
everything that comes close to her?

we talk about lifting our hands in worship, reaching out toward the heavens. but the unloved, the hesitant, the terrified part of me hugs me instead.

no, i will not be vulnerable.

do you know what happened to me, when i was a child, when i raised my arms? do you know what happened to me when i dared look up? to reach? to plead?

reaching was a dangerous thing: it indicated longing. longing was dangerous because it indicated need. need was exploited, need was abused, need was someone else's power over what they could touch.

there is so much i can't do. i feel shame for all of it, for everything that comes more easily for others.

raise your hands, renée. how hard is that? how stupidly hard is that?

it is so hard. it is so terrifying. it is standing before someone unable to protect yourself. it is the inability to cover your soft underparts. it is their giggling, the looks in their eyes, the way you kill yourself in your head because you know you would rather die than live through what they are doing to you. what they are going to do to you.

so many stupid roadblocks, things i can't get past. the despair is huge. the wondering is huge. even as i travel down the road of vulnerability with others, i see that it leads toward more vulnerability with god, because god is in those others, because god is love through those others, and i can't take the others out, can't take them away; they are part of my defense, part of my experimental probing into who god really is.

does god mind that? does this jealous god mind?

god,

i want you to be responsible.
i want it to be my fault.

i want you to be in control.
i want to control you.

i want you big enough to blame.
i want you small and boxed in so i
can only blame me.

i want you scary enough to run
from.
i want you safe enough to trust.

intimacy feels like sin.
intimacy with you feels like sin.

the more i acquainted myself with my sadness, the more i discovered that the symbolism of the church actually described and expressed it.

to me, the stained glass was a story bled in images, in panes. it was church-sanctioned art displayed for a culture that didn't really believe in "art." holiness mixed with sorrow and agony, all blurred and etched three stories above the congregation. there was something magnificent and sacred about these stories without words, these images of faith and hope and longing.

when we took communion, i trembled, feeling the brokenness of christ's body. when others were baptized, i imagined myself plunging beneath the water with them.

the simple cross at the front of the sanctuary spoke more words to my heart than the preacher ever did.

but sermons and bible studies and discussion groups were full of people who tried to explain these things, these symbols. they dissected them and debated them—gave them bullet points and pithy phrases all beginning with the same letter—ultimately reducing them all to nothing. i watched as good people became angry over "wrong doctrine." several left the church because they couldn't find reconciliation. i saw pastors and associates disagree. i watched them form statements and definitions, succinct enough to print on the back of a bulletin, wordy enough to be precise.

i wanted the simplicity of the stained glass, the waters of baptism, the bread and grape juice (we were baptists; we didn't drink wine). i wanted their mystery without explanations, without discussion. i wanted to embrace what they spoke to me and not be forced into what others thought they actually meant.

one summer i was in an intensive spiritual growth program, one of those "become a real christian in three months" deals, with daily memorized bible verses (we had to say them to eat, and they were cumulative—by the end we were quoting three chapters verbatim in order to get a meal), trips to orphanages, daily devotions, daily self-sacrifice, no-pain-no-gain stuff.

it was basically a christian boot camp, and the leader—my associate pastor—was a former police officer, so he ran it with authority and without frills.

we slept in the church basement when we weren't on the bus or on the floor of another church basement in some random city or camping at the foot of mt. ranier (which we'd climbed part of, yes indeed). and every single morning we had to run one mile.

after the first few days i came down with terrible shin splints—really agonizing, splitting pains that shot from my toes all the way up to my knees with every step. i thought i was going to pass out from the pain. but it didn't matter, i still had to run. and praise god while running, too.

we were running foothill trails, and the one rule, the only rule, was that we had to beat our associate pastor in the run. as long as we crossed the metaphysical finish line before him, we were fine.

if we didn't cross the line before he did, we had to run the whole mile again.

there i was, the last one around the bend, biting my lip so hard i tasted blood, praying one phrase over and over in my head: please let me finish, please let me finish, dear god, please let me finish.

i was in the final stretch, my friends were standing by the

bus, and the finish line was in my sight. but i felt something brush my elbow, and a man-made breeze whooshed by.

it was my associate pastor. i watched as he started running as fast as he could—it was deliberate, it was intentional—he actually wanted to humiliate me by beating me.

i watched the other kids cheer for him as he ran up to them, and i felt the despair sink in my heart. i was the only one. i was the last one. i had to run it again.

and so i did.

and i'm still running.

the shadows breathe in me. the darkness fills me up. i cry for the light, for hope, but all feels lost, dark, hopeless.

i've tried to outrun this deadness, this emptiness. i've tried to make myself so busy that it would go away: godstuff, churchstuff, bible studies and worship practice and midweek cell groups—in the end i would tumble into bed exhausted and wrung out, overworked, overdone, and in those moments before sleep, the chasm, the blackness, it all returned.

it stretched out below me in those fleeting, half-light seconds before sleep, taunting me, enticing me to leap into its depths, to let it swallow me up.

i resisted.

i banished it with a prayer, the sign of the cross; i quoted scripture out loud; i cast out imaginary demons.

i fell asleep with the words of god on my lips.

o holy god
your will frightens me.

i plead for this cup to pass
to go beyond my lips
that i might not have to drink of its bitterness
that i might drink instead
from the sweet goblet of certainty and control
of choosing my own path
my own destiny.

i am afraid:
to entrust you with my life
my moments of doubt
the fear i cannot explain.

i am afraid:
to believe that you are good
though i long for it
even in this land of the living
and in the dead places in my own soul.

i am afraid:
to rip open my heart
to offer the contents to you to believe that you will
be gentle with them
with me.

i long to keep my privacies close
my yearnings tucked inward
my loves within my own grasp.

please be kind to my soul.
be kind to my tremblings
be gracious unto me.

i went to christian schools most of my educated life. it started with preschool and ended with my grand dismissal midsemester from a bible college. i remember bible class and weekly chapels and spiritual emphasis weeks.

i always had a crush on the chaplain, whoever he was.

i constantly felt stifled, always felt as if i was unloved. i lived in a christian world that didn't allow freedom. in fact, those in that world were afraid of it. they desperately needed their dots to connect, their questions to get answered, their definitions neat and tidy.

i remember the meeting. it was a dark, hot room, and i was a scared little girl—much younger internally than they knew. all of my scheduled teachers, and some teachers i didn't know very well, were sitting around a big conference-room table.

"we have talked about this student at great length and have come to some conclusions about her. all she wants is attention," the guidence counselor said to the gathered faculty. "do not give it to her. if she comes to you with thoughts of suicide, do not indulge them. come and tell us immediately. you must let us know if she makes threats on her life. it is very important that you do not give her any attention. do not talk to her. do not spend time with her, listen to her, or be alone with her."

in one meeting, the school administration took my safety away. they took away the people who could have helped me, the people who could have shown me love. i don't understand what was so terrible about me to have deserved that. i still have no explanations, no justifications. even in my most hate-filled, self-judgmental moments, my harshest self-loathing moments, i look back on that meeting with confusion, and i feel sad for myself, so very sad for that girl.

she didn't deserve that. she didn't deserve the isolation, the disconnection, the humiliation. instead of trying to figure out what was really going on in my life, instead of trying to define where my pain was coming from, they ignored it. they invented it away, they made it insignificant.

that is part of the problem with tightly controlled christianity. that is the problem with christian schools and christians who do not believe in love or grace, but who depend on their rules to define them, their guilt to guide them, and their actions to purify them.

they cannot let anyone in who is different. they cannot let anyone in who is hurting, who is needy, because those things—the hurt and the need—expose weaknesses in their christian beliefs. the neediness of others points out their own failings, their own hurts, the longings that linger within them, buried and unacknowledged.

i sat in that meeting and wanted to die. i looked at the faces of my teachers and realized they were no longer refuges for me. i didn't want to cry, i didn't want to give them that satisfaction, but i did.

and as i cried, each tear felt like a surrender. each tear added to my humiliation, my feelings of worthlessness. a kind teacher leaned over to offer me a tissue, and the guidence counselor stopped her. "no. let her cry. do not pay attention to her."

my importance, my worth was taken away that afternoon. it was taken in order to protect an image. it was taken to protect an illusion. they didn't want to see the real me. they didn't want to see the brokenhearted, devastated, crushed girl sitting in that chair.

whenever you try to regulate godliness you come up with something a lot less than god. you end up with a sanitized version of half-truths. it looks shiny and it sparkles, but underneath and inside it is decaying and rotting away.

people are too busy trying to keep up the appearances, the sanitation, and they ignore what is beneath. they won't look there. and suddenly, when the foundation gives way, it surprises them. "oh, we didn't know it was so weak, so fragile; we didn't know the foundation had crumbled."

and it always does. the foundation, left untended, left unnoticed, always crumbles. it's just that they were usually too busy worrying about the parts that showed, the parts that other people saw, the exposed parts that defined them to the rest of the world. they couldn't bear to look at what really mattered. and it caused them to miss what was really broken.

i'll never forget the moment i realized i had given up. it was a deadening inside of me, an instant closing off. everything i was, everything that had mattered, was gone.

i remember thinking, even in that moment, "so this is what it's like to harden my heart…" i remember a flash of guilt, a snippet of regret, and then, i remember it now, there was nothing.

i chose to believe that i was better off alone, protected from the ninety-nine, isolated and untouchable. i chose to sit in the wilderness, believing it was my home, struggling to make it comfortable, trying to convince myself that i belonged there.

and i did belong there. i belonged in my desperate aloneness, i belonged in my lack of belonging. my hurt was raw, the damage done to me was real and tangible, a trail of blood showed the woundedness was not just in my imagination.

the loneliness was a comfort, even though i was afraid. whatever happened to me was in my control, my power. whatever pain i felt was now my own fault. there was nothing sticking out for people to tug on, no people to glimpse whatever might be accidentally visible. i felt a sense of happiness simply because so much was lacking. it wasn't that i had died and gone to heaven, but rather that i had died and disappeared, ceased to be, entered a black nothingness that filled me with consolation because it contained nothing. and nothing could hurt me.

i was convinced i would never go back. i knew i didn't belong there.

a moment, frozen. a snippet of memory, a flash of light.

so much hangs in these fragments of time. so much winds itself around each little piece, around each little breath—the unexpected emotion, ragged and raw, and all tangled up.

the trust ebbs and flows, greater in one wave but less in another. i stand back, outside myself, removed from the pain, separated by quiet distance. i watch it as it happens, and i see it all. the protests are swallowed halfway down my throat.

inside, the turmoil, the chaos, the questions. i want to make things better, but i fear the implications of that wish.

how long has it been? how do i go back?

god, father, spirit, i miss you, i miss you, i miss you.

what do you do when you feel like it is happening again? when you see it in slow motion, moving past you as you stand frozen, like molasses, watching each millisecond, unable to stop it, unable to affect it? what do you do when injustice stomps and crushes the weak, defends its arrogance and its decisions? what do you do when you need to run away but there isn't anywhere to go?

community calls me. stronger than therapy, more than medicine—what do i really need? all human beings, all deities hurt you in the end; i know this. it's a matter of degree, a matter of choice. can i accept the hurt, trade it for the pretend fullness? can i fling myself into the void, knowing the bottom is strewn with shards of glass, knowing the bottom might just kill me if i land on it wrong, in an

effort to find something meaningful simply in
the falling?

i want so much more with my life.

i want to make a difference. i want to be the kind of person
i expect others to be. i want community and solitude and
vengeance and justice and mercy and salvation and freedom.

god, father, spirit, i miss you, i miss you, i miss you.

i was hiding under my bed,
pretending that i didn't exist.

he was calling my name,
calling it seductively,
sweetly,

the illusion that i was safe.

i was not safe.

a breath, stifled, squashed down. again.

little hiccups of air, tiny gaspings, baby chokes.

in my family of origin, breathing was dangerous. breathing
meant being caught, found out. breathing was the other one
coming, the fear in my own body, the end of the world.

all these years later, i breathe little breaths. i sneak air into
my body in little chunks, in fragments. i believe somehow
that breath makes me vulnerable, keeps me obvious, exposes
my hiding places.

so much of meditation, of being silent and still, of pursuing
a centered quiet spirituality, is about breath. so much is just
listening to yourself, focusing with each inhale, releasing
with each exhale—breathing becomes a form of prayer.

but when i hear myself breathe, when i hear others breathe,
i am filled with fear. i am overcome with the feeling that
something bad is going to happen, that the boogeyman is
coming, that i will be hurt and abused.

the reality: i desperately crave silence, but i fear it intensely.
when i have it, i don't know what to do with it—i hum
absentmindedly, filling up the spaces, filling up my head.

i want to breathe. i want the breath that anoints the hollow
spaces, the breath that makes me whole.

my first step outside the stifling evangelical fundamentalism i was raised in came from a small episcopal church on the east coast.

it was beautiful (i'm sure that helped). it was made of stone and had stained-glass windows, and the little chapel off to the side was a holy place.

i walked in and felt something i couldn't define or explain— all i could do was weep.

i wept the first 10 or so services, all the way through, from the welcome to the benediction. i bowed my head and allowed the words to flow over me as i cried quietly. i knelt at the rail and took communion, sobbing and unable to meet the priest's eyes.

on the way out, as i passed him, he rested his hand on my shoulder and looked at me.

there was mercy and grace in his touch. there was acceptance and concern in his eyes.

it was the first time i had been allowed to sit in church and acknowledge my pain. it was the first time i had gone before god without pretending, the first time i had dared to be broken and empty and terrified.

i sat in the bathroom with my friend, looking at the stick.

"it's the color of my shorts," i said.

it was pink.

i was pregnant.
i didn't know who the baby belonged to.

was it the boy i was sleeping with every now and then? our noncommittal relationship consisted of furtive clutches under covers and unemotional sex without kissing while depeche mode played in the background. "it's only about the fooling around, the sex," he said. "we're only having a good time. i don't love you."

i said that it was fine, that i didn't want him to love me, that there were no strings.

i lied.

i wanted more than the boy could give me. i wanted forgiveness, redemption, the hope that my sexuality was still mine, that i could still give it away freely, that my father did not own my body, that he did not own me.

who was my aborted child's daddy? who was the one who put the life inside of me—the life i took?

was it my father? i tremble still at the possibility of it. i didn't want to think it, but somehow i knew.

somehow i know.

deadness is more than just what happens to an aborted child. it happens to a woman who feels so wearied from her life that she doesn't care anymore.

i have been that woman. i have been dead and unable to care.

and sometimes, even in this moment lived on the other side of apathy, on the other side of death, i still am.

a choice made,
but not my choice.
angry voices amplify the grief,
explanations given in powerpoint,
in heated rallies,
pro-life proclamations in half-lit church basements.
requiescat in pace
pictures of the dead on the side of trucks,
on sticks held by angry people standing on the corner,
"we will offend you enough to care,
shock you out of your complacency."
look at what you do—look at what you have done
i do not look.
the memories still live in technicolor,
still live in my dreams,
exposed on the table,
false promises,
the choice i couldn't make
but had to.

i grew up with countless sermon illustrations about the god-shaped vacuum—that unfillable hollow part that lurks in every person's gut—that part of us that knows, somehow, that we are wretched and miserable, that we deserve death, that without god we are incomplete.

i spent my life trying to fill that vacuum. i was the perfect example of everything the point was meant to illustrate—busyness, sex, relationships, addictions—i dumped it all in and waited to feel whole.

wholeness never came. i was weak with the longing, the desperateness of being unfulfilled. i felt as if the hole would devour me from the inside, that it would swallow my very self.

god, or my version of him, was the perfect hole-filler. he was tidy, clean, and defined. i prayed repeatedly for holy overflow, for the sense of being full. it became an obsession, a desperate surrender. another. again. on my knees by my bed, hunched over in the pew at church, prayers whispered in the dead of the night.

"fill me."

rules became the god that filled me. thou shalt nots echoed in my head, reminded me of the delicate line between loved and unloved, between full and empty—the precarious balance of living life believing the fullness really came from me, really came from who i was, how i acted, what i did.

but in the quiet of the night, beyond the subscribed solutions, the void remains. the god-shaped vacuum remains.

i have spent my life believing that there was something

wrong with me because of this.

"try harder, let go, give it to jesus, snap out of it, get over it…" there is no room for my longing, no place for my pain.

and all these years and prayers and rededications later, i am as empty as i have ever been.

there have been people in my life who have heard parts of my story and given me advice. they have tried to make me feel better (most of the time i think they are trying to make themselves feel better).

"people only have as much power over you as you choose give them," they say. "leave the past behind, move forward with your life."

my initial response when i hear these things is always guilt: maybe i haven't really done enough. maybe i haven't made the right choices. maybe i don't try as hard as i could.

but i have spent my life trying to move on. i have been in therapy for a very long time. i've been on medications, been admitted to mental hospitals, and prayed for hours with pastors and exorcists. i have talked myself down from ledges. i have made hundreds of promises to myself and to others and to god. i have read my bible over and over again, fasted and prayed, believed and disbelieved and believed again.

i have deliberately made conscious efforts to move forward. i have written up manifestos and memorized scripture. i have tried to let go, i have begged with tears to be cleansed, i have fallen on my face in the bedroom and howled for change.

my healing has only begun to happen when i have been honest with the pain that i have lived. rather than simply putting it behind me, i am finding that i have to befriend it. rather than choosing to forget what happened, i am finding that i must choose to remember.

at dawn he appeared again in the temple courts, where all the people gathered around him, and he sat down to teach them.

the teachers of the law and the pharisees brought in a woman caught in adultery. they made her stand before the group and said to jesus, "teacher, this woman was caught in the act of adultery. in the law moses commanded us to stone such women. now what do you say?" they were using this question as a trap, in order to have a basis for accusing him.

but jesus bent down and started to write on the ground with his finger. when they kept on questioning him, he straightened up and said to them, "if any one of you is without sin, let him be the first to throw a stone at her." again he stooped down and wrote on the ground.

at this, those who heard began to go away one at a time, the older ones first, until only jesus was left, with the woman still standing there. jesus straightened up and asked her, "woman, where are they? has no one condemned you?"

"no one, sir," she said.

"then neither do i condemn you," jesus declared. "go now and leave your life of sin."

john 8:2-11

the associate pastor came up to me. "hey," he said, "your dad called. your mom is in town. you have been excused to go see her."

i paled. my mother was the root of all of my father's evil, all of my evil. it was my fault she had left, and now she was back, and i was still bad. i had to see her? what if i drove her away again? what if she didn't love me? what if i still wasn't good enough?

i jumped up, ran out of the building and across a courtyard and down a bunch of steps into the library where my bible study met. i flopped down, the tears came, and i couldn't stop them. i knew i needed to stop them, knew this vulnerability would get me into trouble—but all i could do was cry.

i cried a long time. finally one of the adult leaders came and found me. she placed a hand on my back and said, "come back, please." my eyes were red and swollen, and i felt as if i were sick—sicker than i'd ever been. i took her hand and walked with her. as i entered the room, i saw that everyone was looking at me. my associate pastor began talking.

"we need to pray for renée who has to see her mother today. renée has always had problems with her mother, with hating her, with being unable to forgive her for leaving, and for blaming her mom for her own problems. i believe that if renée can only forgive her mother and love her, renée will be okay. we're going to pray for renée, that she can do this."

suddenly the group moved forward like a giant flesh-eating amoeba and a bunch of hands were outstretched toward me. the leaders all laid hands on my body—my shoulders, my back. i found myself crying again, though i didn't want to. in spite of the noise of the prayers and the mumbling around me, i found myself hearing my dad in my head:

"please make renée good so her mom will come back."

the group prayed for a long time, and after they finally said amen and released me, i looked up and past the people, and saw my father. he was wearing his long white-sleeved dress shirt, and he was standing there with a smug smile on his face. i saw him lock eyes with the associate pastor and nod.

that day i met my youngest sister for the first time and tried desperately to connect with the mother i had never really known. i found myself standing in a room with her and not knowing what to say. i wanted to ask her if she would come back, wanted to ask her if i could ever be good enough, but instead i said nothing.

when i arrived back at the church that night, they held a special group meeting. they stood me in front of them, expectation on their faces, and asked me how it went. i felt my insides sink. i felt my heart freeze over. and then i lied. i forgave her, i said. i told her i loved her.

they praised jesus for my turnaround the rest of the summer.

my christian life has always been full of the formulated: seven ways to know i am saved, 10 perfect steps to the christian life, five marks of an effective disciple. everything always comes with an agenda. everything has a marked path, a defined journey. everything has a tidy answer.

when i ran away from the church, it was because i was overwhelmed by the packaging. i had no place to be real. i had no place to be broken. my little world had no belonging among them.

it took a few months for the sadness to really approach me. i had left the church feeling tired and wounded but unable to feel the depths of my grief. i kept making excuses for what had happened, kept explaining it away. i blamed myself: i had been too sensitive, too demanding, too needy.

but without the church, i didn't know who i was. my years of being in the front row, of teaching sunday school and playing the harp and being a dutiful christian girl, had defined me. without those roles i felt as if i were simply taking up space in the world, not contributing to any great plan, not making any kind of difference.

even worse, i had left god behind.

god had become an extension of them, their words echoed in my head as his. their perceptions and judgments became what god thought of me. everything i believed dangled from the thread of a god just like them.

i was afraid of that god, certain he had rejected me, too.

i had to get my life together before god could love me. i had to quiet the screaming desperation inside, the emptiness that cried out constantly for satisfaction. i had to find some kind of relief so that i could return to church whole and satisfied, fully consumed.

many people in my life didn't understand why i left the church. my pain had not happened to them, my disappointment was not theirs. they looked at the chaos of my life and blamed my lack of church attendance.

"if you only went to church, you would have friends, be loved, know god, find truth, be free."

the reality was that the path away from church was part of my journey toward the real god.

i could never know the real god without leaving the god of the church. i could never have quieted the voices of those who had condemned me, those who had judged me, humiliated me, shamed me, silenced me, without escaping to where i could hear another voice, a voice without affiliation or denomination, a voice from beyond time.

"neither do i condemn you."

i long for those words to ring true in me. i ache for a feeling, for one moment, of living without feeling condemned. i ache for this love that i sense exists but that i cannot seem to grasp.

god,
who i am is based on what you think of me
(what i have been told you think of me).
though i long for the freedom
of being someone different, something different,
i am terrified of it
because if you think anything else,
if you think anything differently,
there is nothing to hold me up.

i have built my worldview
on things i have thought you have been.
what you have said, what you have done,
how you have thought of me.

i have built myself as a reaction to that,
subconscious or deliberate,
intentional or involuntary.
i am who i am,
and some part of it
is based on the abuse,
based on what he said i was,
what he said you said i was.

to hear myself with these words
that call to my soul,
to think of myself that way,
is to rewrite everything i am.
who i am is invalid.
it is based on a lie.

though i hate who i am,
how i am,
it is comfortable.
it is who and how i have lived
all these years.

the stained-glass windows in the episcopal church were very women-friendly, and they touched something in me that felt invalidated and ashamed of my girlness. sometimes as the speakers were talking, my brain focused on the woman in the front-right pane. her hands were full of gifts, offering, and there was such rapture on her face. i thought: i would love to love my god like that.

as part of our connection with god, we read the following passage over and over:

"suppose one of you has a hundred sheep and loses one of them. does he not leave the 99 in the open country and go after the lost sheep until he finds it? and when he finds it, he joyfully puts it on his shoulders and goes home. then he calls his friends and neighbors together and says, 'rejoice with me; i have found my lost sheep.' i tell you that in the same way there will be more rejoicing in heaven over one sinner who repents than over 99 righteous persons who do not need to repent."

at one point the facilitator asked us to think and journal about what we felt, about what would happen, if we were the sheep waiting for the shepherd, and we saw him coming: what would he say? where were we? how would we react?

i sat in that church, sprawled on the floor, leaning against a sturdy pillar with my eyes closed, trying to imagine that moment, trying to be that sheep.

my mind showed me a dusty, dark place. i was alone, it was quiet. there was only the occasional moaning of the wind. there were no birds, there was no shade.

i heard the shepherd coming a long way off. he was whistling.

"hey," he said to me. "i have missed you. i am so glad i found you."

he extended a hand to wipe my tear-stained, dusty cheeks.

"come back with me," he said. "come back to the others."

i shook my head and pulled away.

"no," i said.

he looked surprised, but it did not change the immense compassion on his face.

"no," i said again. "i can't go back. i don't want to. i don't trust the other 99. i don't want to be hurt again. please don't make me be hurt again."

the shepherd sat down on the ground next to me.
"okay," he said quietly. "i'll just stay here with you then..."

the shepherd waited with me
for a long time.

there was so much that was shattered and broken in me. i was distrustful and skeptical, and i pushed love away because i was terrified of it. the thought of being hurt kept me from taking risks, and kept my life protected and safe.

my husband came into my life with great gentleness. he never forced his way in. he never insisted that i give him anything that i couldn't give. he simply sat with me and waited with me and loved me.

i learned from him the wonder of being loved.

he has stayed with me even when i have begged him to leave. he has respected me even when i have yelled at him and thrown things at him and refused to respect myself. he has held me when there were no words to be said, knowing that to say them would only trivialize my pain.

he walked with me through the process of intense therapy, of nights when i slept in the bathtub or the closet, too terrified to be with another person; too full of memories to be in my own bed. he has watched me sign "no suicide" contracts and visited me in mental hospitals. he has nurtured the small wounded parts of me and always believed i would make it.

i have held on to his hope for me when i have had none for myself. i have held on to his love for me when i have felt unloved and afraid. through him i have learned that there are places in me that love can reach. through him i have been willing to begin to be loved. through him i learned the worth of letting people in. because of him i began to open up to others again, to be brave.

he has been the beginning of my ability to believe.

water is a friend to the grief in my soul.

water was the solace, the comfort, for the dry places in my heart.

sometimes i sit at the harbor and drink up the waves.
there is a bench on the edge of the jetty, overlooking the ocean. fierce, huge waves pound the surf and splash white foam over the rocks.

i lick my lips. they taste like salt.

the healing rhythm of the sea. relentless, persistent, the waves have been ebbing in and out forever—since the beginning of the world they have slammed against the sad shoreline, dwindled out quietly, and then slammed back in again.

it's an enormous truth: as life goes on, as i walk and fret and worry and live, the waves continue. they are predictable, sacred with expectancy. i find some healing and comfort in them.

so much of me finds some connection to wholeness when i am soaking up the wind, the salt, the movement of the sea.

i stood near the front of the bus, trembling. the associate pastor towered over me. i was wearing my official choir dress; the choir was preparing to perform at a church nearby.

"you are making me look like a fool," he said, bending down so his face was in front of mine. "you are telling all my friends that you want to kill yourself. stop. stop wanting so much attention."

tears welled up in my eyes, a huge sadness sat in the pit of my stomach. i felt myself shrivel up inside, felt the familiar feeling of shame.

the rest of the choir stood in a line by the side door of the church, watching. i didn't want to cry in front of him, didn't want to admit my pain, so i stood there, my hands clenched, my chin up, waiting for him to let me pass.

soon he did, and i made my way across the parking lot, into the church and over to the harp. as i began to play, hot humiliated angry tears flew from my eyes and landed on the strings. my fingers slipped and sloshed. i couldn't hide; my pain was exposed and naked in front of the entire congregation and the rest of the choir. my associate pastor stood near the door, his arms crossed over his body, smiling.

—

it's worth making the distinction between god and church, but it is a difficult distinction for me.

i was never allowed an independent god.

my god was formulated by the men around me. my god was given to me on a silver platter: take, eat, do this in remembrance of the god we give you.

i know that the right thing to do is to rip it apart, to pull out the men from the god, but i can't do it. they are intertwined together, they are so very much the same.

i must spend time with each aspect of god, with each aspect of the men, untangle the knots, tear apart the associations. i must believe there can be a parting; i must believe there can be a way.

o *ruach elohim*,
feminine
spirit of god who
pushes back darkness
chaos

leaving space
for birth
for creation.

o *ruach*,
feminine
spirit of god who
breathes out hope
life

making space
for safety
for untangling knots
for creating
new paths.

o *ruach*,
feminine
spirit of god
i beg you
please
hold me.

i began working at a christian company in the midst of great confusion about my christianity.

i believed in the purpose of the company and what they did—if there was ever a place where i could be with my doubts, it was in this place—but i always struggled with feeling that my lack of faith kept me on the outer fringes.

it was never anything anyone said, and i don't even know that anyone really knew, but i felt like i was separated, isolated in my inability to believe.

i started spending time in the company chapel, a little room with candles and pillows and crosses. i didn't go in there with a specific purpose. at first i went because it was dark and quiet and i felt safe. i played with the pastels and the blank journals, dimmed the lights, and breathed in the scent of the candles while listening to quiet instrumental music.

my thoughts wandered inevitably to god. i felt like i was bad because i wasn't going to church, because i had deliberately walked away. people in my life told me that many of my family's problems were caused because we weren't going to church, and it weighed on me. guilt.

but i couldn't go. i couldn't make myself walk through the doors of a church. i wasn't ready for that.

in the chapel, though, with its dim lights and candles and my crayon drawings, i felt like i was connecting with god. i felt in some strange way like i was going to church, that i was having church, that i found an entrance into god's presence that felt like something holy.

the more i discovered myself being willing to be with god, the more i was filled with hesitancy. i was accepting a god that accepted me, and i felt like i was always looking over my shoulder. "are you sure you mean me, god? are you sure i belong here?"

each moment spent in the chapel felt both safe and terrifying. each captured second of safety flooded me with an insecurity that it would all be snatched away, that i was taking something i didn't deserve, something i couldn't have.

—

i remember a time when i was feeling suicidal. i wanted to run away. i wanted to go to where i had been the happiest. i wanted to find some inner courage to stop hurting the people i loved, somehow, to remove myself enough from them so they could put the pieces of themselves and our family back together again.

i drove and drove. i drove to the harbor, and on the way i prayed for a miracle. please, if there is anything worthy in me that can be saved, please, i want a miracle.

the second i stepped out of the car, the salty ocean smell hit me, and i began to cry my own salty tears. i slung my leather backpack over my shoulders and started walking toward an ocean viewpoint—i knew there was a bench overlooking the water just waiting for me.

as i rounded the corner of a very big construction area (wondering if it was worth the trudge), i began to hear them. cries, squawks, dark shadows of wings soared over the ground.

i stopped at the edge of the cliff, almost to my chosen bench, and gasped. there, in front of me, covering the rocks, filling every space of the water as far as I could see, were pelicans.

hundreds of them.

as i sat down on the bench, watching in amazement, a couple walked up to me and smiled. "look at that," they said, "it's a miracle."

i sat there watching the pelicans for about an hour and a half. it was mystical and magical, and as the darkness started to fall i walked around and gathered a handful of little stones, a bit of a seashell, some tangible reminder of what had happened to me.

for me.

i called a friend and said, "do you hear them? do you hear them crying? they are crying my tears, they are calling out my pain."

i am finding myself engulfed in a love that simply will not let me go. i am discovering that the grace and the hope that i have wanted so desperately, that i have ached for, is beginning to emerge in little things i never noticed. sometimes it takes a big thing to smack me upside the head—a magnification of a lot of little things—"look here, dork," it says, "i'll give you a lot of detail so you can see how much of it you're missing. then, when you're feeling despair, you can look for the little things and see them as magnificent."

i'd always thought that hope took the form of lightning bolts or blazing fires or northern lights. for me it's just like emily dickinson wrote: "hope is the thing with feathers." hope is a giant flock of pelicans.

hope is love and grace and light even in the middle of the shadow of death.

—

i discovered my first gender-inclusive bible in the early '90s.

i started reading, and it was as if i was reading something that included me for the first time in my life. i knew that i had felt degraded and dismissed as a woman in the church: i had lived it. i knew that the language of the people around me had enforced those feelings—the words were full of *men* and *father,* and the examples were always of men and fathers—but i hadn't even noticed on any conscious level how the bible itself had excluded me. it was such a part of my life, of my memorization, of everything i was, i didn't even notice.

the priest from the episcopal church on the east coast—the priest who had watched me cry every sunday during the service—gave me the inclusive bible. he honored the worth of women, and knew the necessity of portraying that in words from the pulpit. somehow he also knew that my tears came from feeling isolated and degraded and dismissed.

i opened the bible cautiously. it was a version i had never heard of before. i had been through all the classes on translation at bible college. i knew about formal and dynamic equivalence, i knew the proper translations for good baptists, and some part of me felt like a heretic for daring to venture outside the officially sanctioned evangelical translations.

but that afternoon, i started reading. i started with passages in the new testament, passages i had always known, passages i had memorized. as i read, i felt something soften in me, something that had been long hardened and closed off and isolated.

brothers and sisters...

those simple words brought belonging to me. suddenly i was

included. suddenly i mattered.

that bible changed me. i wept with the joy and inexpressible gratitude for realizing that i was included.

i came to realize that even the scriptures used in my childhood had been like a stream of water dripping continuously on a rock. over time it had worn the surface away. i hadn't even known it was there, i hadn't even noticed, but that unobtrusive little trickle had changed the rock forever.

i sat nervously in front of the inner-city church, clutching my purse and staring into the distance. christian salsa music was blaring over an old speaker set up at the corner of the parking lot, and the sound was tinny and distorted.

i'd come for spiritual direction, an elusive term that, in spite of its obscurity, seemed to pinpoint precisely what i needed.

what i need, still.

she is wonderful. she has beautiful hands and safe eyes. she has a smile that lights up her face.

i entered the darkness of the church and sat on an old chair, fidgeting. she was simply silent, waiting and watching.

within moments the tears came.

and she allowed me them. i felt no judgment, no hurry to be well, no embarrassment at my brokenness.

sitting with her, i felt god was willing to watch my pain, to acknowledge it.

she gave god a space to be with me, and i discovered that he was.

late at night when the world was dark and still and quiet, i
bundled in my warmest clothes and walked to the episcopal
church on the other end of town. the sound of my boots
crunching on the snow sounded loud to the world of quiet
late-night silence. i walked past apartments with their
windows lit up, and the sense of homelessness in me spilled
out in tears that had no words. i wanted light, warmth,
a feeling of safety. i wanted what i never had, the home i
never had been able to find.

there was something incredibly comforting about reaching
the church. i sat under its eaved protection, leaned
against the sturdiness of its cold stone walls, wrapped my
arms around myself, and sobbed. i felt safe to cry in that
place, and somehow i knew god was there, even in those
frozen, breathless seconds, even from the other side of the
sanctuary, separated from the candles, from the cross, from
the old wooden pews. i called for him in the dark; in the
silence i clasped my mittened hands in prayer, lifting them
up in yearning, bowing my head with despair and loneliness.

in the highest moments of my disconnection and the
deepest moments of my sadness, i stood and walked to
the patches of snow in front of the side chapel door. with
tears streaming down my cheeks, pain and sorrow causing
my body to shake, i lay down in the snow. slowly and
deliberately, but with great desperation, i made a snow
angel. it was like a sacrament: an imprint of my presence,
a sign of seeking, a cry for connection. lord god, hear my
prayer. then i walked, exhausted, back to my apartment.

the next morning, in the fresh sunlight, as the snow began
to melt and the world came back to life, i returned to the
church on the corner. the world was so different in the
daylight, the noise of traffic and people cluttered my insides.

i clenched my fists. as inconspicuously as possible, i stood by the little restaurant across the street and looked at my angel, still lying there in the snow. it gave me a sense of pleasure, of purpose, to see it there. it was as if i had left a part of me at the church, the part of me that was aching and wounded and unable to go on another moment. it was as if i had been willing to be vulnerable with something bigger than me, but barely: willing only in silence, only in darkness, only when no one else was watching, only when no one else could hurt me. my angel in the snow spoke the words i could not speak to another human soul.

its presence called out, "someone was here. someone was seeking. someone was willing to be vulnerable. someone still believed, even in her darkest moments of unbelief."

the beginning of my hope came in the form of a little girl.

a little girl named jordan. my daughter.

this hope didn't come easily or instantly. it wasn't that
i was given a daughter, and she redeemed me simply by
her presence. it wasn't as if i finally found my destiny as a
mom, an instant connection with my own motherlessness, a
sudden purpose in my pain.

in fact, i never had that connection. i never felt intimately
fulfilled, i never felt completely satisfied. for a long time, as a
mother, i felt like a failure.

my daughter's birth was the beginning of a journey. it
is, and has been, a journey through despair and fear and
confrontation, a journey through hope and faith and belief,
a journey that has ultimately brought me the ability to be
with honest with god.

honesty birthed hope in me.

it created for me the ability to be myself and still have some
kind of relationship with god. it allowed me my human
frailty, my confusion, my sadness—everything that i had
pushed away in my attempts to be more spiritual.

it was almost like something physical had always been in
the way of my belief. i heard the words others spoke to me,
i threw down my misconceptions, opened my heart to the
truth, talked myself through the fear, and yet belief still did
not come.

the more i tried, the more i made an effort, the more i attempted to push my reality away, to "get over it," to move on, the more stuck i was. the more despair lodged into my heart and made its home there. the more the brokenness sunk into my bones.

there was no forcing it.

relief came to me through honest dialogue. conversations with my spiritual director, discussions with my husband, with a friend—the more i talked, the more the frightened places in me opened up. the more the doubt was allowed to express itself, the more it eased away. the more i was able to express my pain, the more valid my hurt became.

but i was still fragile. my faith was still easily betrayed.

i recently entered a christian bookstore for the first time in about 10 years.

funny how numb the brain gets to absurdity, how easily we swallow the asinine.

back in high school and college i was a devout christian bookstore addict. for me it was mostly about the music—i was a fan of christian music (particularly the edgier stuff like the 77s, daniel amos, crumbacher, steve taylor, etc.), and there was no organized internet or online shopping at the time, so physically walking into the store was the only way to go.

have these stores gotten worse in the past few decades?

i ask this because i walked in and was repulsed by what i saw there. christian candy and "bars of judah" (fancy god-labeled granola stuff) and fortune cookies with scripture verses inside. veggie tales action figures and puzzles and games and christian coffee and dumb bumper stickers and key chains and row upon row of inane kids' stuff.

it was sickening. i stood in the middle of this huge room, surrounded by godstuph, and i wanted to weep. and scream. and barf. i was furious and disgusted and horrified and brokenhearted all at the same time.

i wanted to tear it all down, to rip it to shreds, to stop it. i wanted to run up to my fellow browsers, shake them, and scream, "don't you see? don't you see? this isn't it! this isn't it!" it was everything wrong with the church, everything

wrong with trying to market jesus, market testaMINTS and
godly lemon drops and christian chocolate, trying to wrap
the gospel, the passion, the life, the god without limits into
something tantalizing and tasty and understandable.
isn't the wonder of god, of jesus, that they are beyond our
ultimate understanding? isn't the mystery part of the story?
isn't the unknowing part of what makes it so beautiful?
i want the wild god—the god who spends time with
people nobody else will look at: the insane, the ugly, the
disenfranchised, the hurt.

oh god jesus spirit, lover of my soul, author of
life, friend of the friendless—give me the raw
fiery passionate you, the one i can stand in awe
of, the one bigger than my attempts to rein you
in. surprise me, give me unabashed, undiluted,
unmarketed grace. have mercy on me.

soft light filters through the windows; it's muted, as if it's shining through gauze. my daughter and i snuggle together on the bed, counting to 10, making our fingers into airplanes, tickle bugs, playful monsters. her eyes are bright, her smile is real, and i feel the hardness around my heart soften as she grabs my hand and giggles. "mama," she says. "you too."

(this means "i love you.")

i want to freeze this moment in my memory, every single piece of it. the smell of the candles near the doorway. the way the light illuminates the red in her hair. the way the quilt wraps around my legs, protective and soft.

i stroke her forehead, brush the hair off her face, and she has such a look of contentment that for a moment i feel a pang of my own loss.

that old pang, that old hurt, the neverending longing for family, for community. i was ashamed. the despair oozed out of me back then.

the loneliness was deeper than i could have ever been. more intense than i ever was.

my daughter curls into me, sleeping. her fingers twitch slightly, her mouth flickers. she's dreaming. i wrap my arm around her and kiss her eyelid. then i fall asleep, too, thankful for home.

"you come across as someone who is so together," my spiritual director told me. "you seem so okay that i have to consciously remember that there's a tempest underneath the surface."

"i hold my pain very close to me," i said. "it's not something i let other people see."

"thank you for sharing your pain with me," she replied.

i was so grateful for her words; for the freedom she gave me to feel.

i want a multilayered god.
i want a god of art, of music,
of old icons, of ancient prayers.

i want a god who is able to be
bigger than i can imagine,
a god beyond my comprehensions
and limited definitions.

i want a home.
a place to feel at home,
a safe place,
a refuge
to work out my salvation
with fear and trembling.

a safe place
to be able to risk everything
to surrender everything,
to find that i'm not alone
when those i let go of
crumble in pieces
around me.

it took us two years to realize our daughter was different.

i'm sure part of it was denial, part of it was new parenthood, and part of it was reckless hope.

when we were presented with evidence we could no longer deny, i was spun into an intense cycle of desperation and anger. it was mostly about my ego: my husband and i had talked about having a child with our combined wit, humor, and intelligence. we had fantasized about our child's future: enrolled in the best college, vying for the presidency, creating something wonderful, *time* magazine's person of the decade.

our ideals were shattered when we realized jordan's limitations, and it hurt. it hurt my pride. it hurt my ego. and it infuriated me.

"haven't i been through enough in my life?" i asked god in my moments of undiluted honesty. "haven't you done enough to me? haven't i been given more than i can bear?"

we were confused and frightened and sad. it wasn't that we didn't love jordan or that we cared for her less, but rather that we didn't understand what we had done wrong, why we had been given imperfection.

we wanted her to become what we were hoping for. we didn't want her to be "different."

i haven't always been the best mom to my daughter. i have screwed up at times. badly. i have wanted her to be someone she isn't. i have hurt her with my words and with my attitude.

but i have also learned how to love someone unconditionally. i have learned how it feels to look at someone and know that you would do anything for her.

i have sang with her and danced with her and twirled in circles with her until i fell down.

we have celebrated every little triumph with jordan. we have laughed with her, shed tears with her, and praised her accomplishments.

we have learned that we do not always know what is good for us.

i never before understood parents who, like martyrs, talked about their disabled children. with tears in their eyes they said they were blessed to have the kids they did, that they learned a lot about god and life as a result of them.

but now i understand. our honest truth is that our family is better because of our daughter, exactly as she is. we are stronger people. we are more tolerant people. i have experienced what it feels like to have to take my hands off any control over my daughter's life. i have learned to try to take my hands off the controls of my own life, too. i have learned that i can't rush time or fate or destiny. i have learned that my little girl was given to me, and even though it is frustrating and exhausting and sometimes overwhelming, there was something i needed to learn from her. there is much i have not yet learned.

there is so much i am still learning.

i stopped seeing my spiritual director after september 11.

although the cessation was sudden, the decision was not. my initial reaction to the attacks, as with so many others, was shock, disbelief—a bright and blinding overwhelm that seized my insides and twisted them, that took my sense of security and stripped it completely away.

i was safe, then i was unsafe, then i was a child and unsafe, then i realized how unsafe i'd always been.

as i watched the world in the days after the attacks, as words and ideologies and "sides" began to emerge, i found myself slipping away. i found myself entering a place of rage and despair, a place that had no room for seeking or clarity or spirituality. the mystical side of me was driven underground; it felt betrayed, ashamed. the part of me that was full of longing, desperate and thirsty and barren and deserted, was forced beneath the surface.

more and more the world split into black and white, religious definitions, claimed battleground: god on one side; allah on the other. and as each proclaimed loudly how different they were, with speeches, with waving flags, with suicide bombs, they began to look exactly the same.

i began to battle with something far, far beyond "why do bad things happen to good people?" frankly i didn't care; at that moment i was disillusioned, broken. i felt no one was good, that nothing was deserved or owed. my crusade became something more than the curiosity, the strangeness, the wrongness of human suffering, and rather became something else. something deeper. something that resonated all the way back to my childhood, to the first time i was raped by my father; to the first time he sang hymns to me and touched my breasts.

why does god allow his name to be used to justify evil?

where is god's sense of dignity—god's sense of self-worth? with all the evil in the world, all the horrible ugly things people do to each other, i can understand in some theological christian education-type sense that people are given the freedom to choose. and, on some level, i very much respect that.

at the same time, you'd think the free will would come with a caveat from god: "hey honey, you wanna be an idiot or a creep or a child molester—fine. that's your choice. just don't drag my name into it. don't speak for me."

for years, countless moments, i have been told what god thinks. i have been given this neat little box, with neon shiny edges, clearly defined lines, and i've been told exactly how to be to make god like me. i've been given the answers in the form of moralities, in do & don't printable versions, in nifty little catch phrases and cutesy alliterative sayings. i am so tired of other people defining god for me. i am so tired of people claiming to speak for god, claiming to tell me just exactly what i need to do, what i should be and think. what i should pursue.

when the war on terrorism here took on this whole "god bless america" mentality, this whole "evildoers" and "justice" and "prevail" language, it triggered some part of me that only wanted to run away. run from god, run from the thought of god, run from any kind of a god who allowed himself to let people speak for him.

---

i think that my experience with the terrorist attacks here finally helped me to see the magnitude of how people, even people from varying religious beliefs, claimed to speak for god.

it had always been a very private struggle. i knew that my father had dictated god's will to me, that he had contorted god's words to suit his own purposes. i knew that the church i grew up in had tried to tell me what god wanted, and how he planned to accomplish what he wanted in my life.

the terrorist manifesto showed me that i needed to find out about god independently if i was to understand him at all. it showed me that most humans (not just those in my realm of existence) have an agenda, that they see god the way they want to see him, and they can make him say anything they wish in order to defend whatever they happen to believe.

i began to explore god for myself, and in that process, at about the time i had given up on church altogether, god brought a friend into my life. this friend never claimed to speak for god; in fact, he didn't say much of anything about god to me at all.

he lived god's love into me through his life, through his love. he cared about me, was willing to spend time with me, and embraced me in all of my fractured disbelief and doubt. he didn't give me pat answers. in fact, many times he didn't give me any answers. rather he gave me permission to be without them—an indescribable gift. he gave me the space to ask questions, to be honest, to struggle, to grieve.

i felt the freedom to be half-finished. i felt the freedom to cry, to mourn for all i had lost. i felt that god loved me in the midst of my half-finished mourning, that he heard me when i cried. i felt that love through my friend, a love that was gentle and patient and playful.

my friend is a pastor, but he didn't bring god back to me with words. he didn't just preach hope and life, he lived it.

he lives it still.

he helped bring life and hope to me. he saw my deadness and my brokenness and entered into it instead of trying to talk me out of it. he acknowledged my despair and then quietly, without words, pointed the way to something bigger than him. he pointed me to springtime and light and life, all the while acknowledging the winter, the darkness, the pain.

my friend has his own stories; he wears his own scars. but through them he has remained honest and real and raw. i have seen him, through everything, as a person, as someone who is able to be fallible, and hurting, and human. in his humanity, he has helped me to see the humanity of jesus.

he has been jesus to me. he has represented god to me without words, given me a god i could feel safe with, a god reflected in him that was approachable. he showed me a god who honors even my unbelief, who values my struggles, my questions, and even my doubts; a god who loves me, as i am, in the fullness of my brokenness.

me: broken and wounded and still seeking. me: full of flame and water, hope and despair, belief and disbelief.

me: broken and bruised, but desiring desperately to be whole.

isn't it something that somebody like me can begin to come to life again, to dare

to believe again, to hope for redemption again?

isn't it something that these stories matter? that my story and his story and your story intertwine and meet, and that god makes something lovely and beautiful and meaningful out of our wretched, halting words?

i love the feeling of emerging, the way it feels when i find myself coming out of the darkness into the light...everything is so much sweeter and more vibrant. little things become stunningly beautiful and that which has been taken for granted becomes unbelievably precious.

i was always terrified of silence.

because silence was full of possibility. of good and of bad. but in silence i could create my own reality. i could stand quietly outside of the definitions others had placed upon me and be whoever i wanted.

silence was also full of memory, of the noises of the past.

silence was full of me.

in the quiet stillness, as i offered myself to god, i heard my internal voices clearly—all of their judgments, their self-condemnation, their self-hatred. the doubt and bitterness and anger had no distraction, no safe place to hide.

i went on retreats that emphasized silence simply to place myself in this predicament, to quiet myself long enough to find out who i really was underneath the busyness, the external noise.

it was never comfortable. when i stripped away all of my stuff, i never liked the coward that lurked beneath. i found myself silent before god, trembling, not knowing what to say or how to approach the holiness i saw unveiled to me. i found myself silent and uncomfortable, seeking noise in any form i could find it, proof i was not alone.

i went to a monastery. i went to the services in the church and soaked the chants into me, let them wash over my broken spirit. i walked the prayer path, trudged through the mud and weeds, stopped at each station of the cross to think.

as i walked i noticed that i was finding myself drawn to the people in the background. i began watching the people around jesus, noticed their faces, their expressions, studied how they reacted to him. one of the stations showed a woman in obvious pain. she stood slightly hunched with her hands over her face, and i was startled as i realized: that is me, that is me, that is me.

i finished the path with tears in my eyes, a little disconcerted, a little unsettled.

i returned to the monastic living quarters, and there, in my sparse room, in moments of silence, with the window open to the sunshine and the ocean air, i discovered anew how angry i was. how lonely i was. how frightened i was.

there is so much i want to believe—both about god and about myself. there is so much in me that feels noble, that feels brave. i like to think that sometimes i know who i am and how to live in this world, apart from all of my desperate unbelief.

but when i sit for a moment in silence and breathe in the quiet, i am flattened by who i really am. i am flattened by what i really think of god—by the emotions that rise up, the loneliness, the fury.

underneath everything, even this book, even these words, there is a woundedness that has no description. there is fundamental damage, a crack in the foundation.

the more i seek little things, the more i see the holiness in them.

my daughter had lunch with me at work, and at the time i was paranoid about how much she was bothering people. i had this agenda, my father's agenda, in the back of my head: "children should be seen and not heard, quiet, quiet." and all i could think about was how important it was that she be quiet and not disturb people and "ssh! it's an office!" then as i went to hug her, i caught a whiff of her amazing little girl smell, the scent of her hair and her baby shampoo and the simple smell of her, and the tears came and i hated myself for wasting those moments with her, for being worried about what other people thought.

i hated myself for wanting to silence her, to make her be good, to behave, and i kissed her on the forehead, and she smiled and patted my cheek and i was so glad for her, for me, for us. i was so thankful for the little bit of grace that is wrapped up and encompassed in my beautiful daughter, and i promised myself that i would allow that grace, the grace of her, to seep through the dry, crusty places in me and bring me refreshment and sanctity and holiness. i promised never ever to let that grace get away.

and suddenly, oh so suddenly, i see
this amazing newness around me.

i see the ways in which something divine and sacred is squirming itself into my soul, and it frightens me but it exhilarates me at the same time, and i think: yes! i might be loved. yes! i might matter. yes! there is something bigger than me, wiser than me, and yes! i am caught in its grip in a hundred different ways—it's like my life is integrating and shaping itself and closing the holes and making sense for the first time ever! and yes! i like it there.

i like it in this little space of being loved.

i like this newness, this fresh perspective, this ordinary holiness weaving itself into the tapestry of my life, and i want to worship something; i want to proclaim my gratitude, my awe, the miracle that i *notice,* that i see what's happening. i want to hold out my hands and say "thank you."

i want to tell the world that something is fundamentally shifting in me, and i don't understand it, but it feels like rebirth, like new roots in old soil, it feels like hope and light. i want to tell the world that this thing i have sought for so long is coming home to me in spite of myself; that i am being relentlessly pursued by a benevolent light-filled grace that i can't explain or define or resist.

i want to tell the world that my father was wrong, that i am greater than what happened to me, that i am greater than all the shame and wrong that i have done.

i want to tell the world that i see pelicans and light and holiness everywhere I look.

and i am!

i am loved. i am beginning to believe it. i am trying to embrace the love coming from that which i do not know; that which i've always been afraid of.

we were early, or the sunday school teacher was late, and in those endless molasses-timed minutes i didn't know what to do with myself.

the others standing around shook my hand, shook my hand again, we made small talk with a few people, and then i ran away.

out, out, out of the foyer—into the welcoming outside air, a set of steps under a shade tree, i sat, breathing hard, shaking a little, asking myself out loud, "why am i doing this again? why am i doing this?"

muttering to myself, under the tree, on the second to the top step, huddled over my familiar bible, rolling a chunk of yellow clay around in my fingers, i found myself again. felt the ground under my feet, played with blades of grass near my left side, looked away from the people filing into the nearby building.

i tried to quiet my heart, tried to give myself safety, a sense of self and security from within me, something not dependent on anything or anyone else. i tried to find my face, the one i wear when i'm scared, the big smile, the frozen feigned interest, the one that gets me through.

it wasn't there. i couldn't find the face, couldn't find the heart to wear it. i wanted to be real, to be exactly me.

time passed and suddenly my husband was calling my name. i felt paralyzed. i couldn't move, couldn't even find breath. standing up felt like impossible effort, mingling with people felt like certain extinction.

i wanted my candles and my solitude and the darkness. i wanted the obscurity of the floor.

but i walked in, holding my husband's hand tightly,

squeezing my daughter's shoulders. we sat down in the very last row, right side, on the corner. it was easy access to the exit. far away from conversation.

i watched the whole thing. i listened the whole time. i sat dumbly through the worship songs (i didn't know a single one) and cowered and cringed at certain phrases, but i stayed and watched and listened.

i stayed. even though everything in me wanted to run away, to hide, to bury myself in my own relationship with god, my own desperate seeking, my own pathetic longing, that which is beyond my own words.

i watched. even though i wasn't sure of what i was looking at. sometimes i closed my eyes to see.

i listened. even though it made me vulnerable, even though it exposed a part of myself; even though the words hurt at times.

there was relief in leaving as the service ended. i rushed toward the door gasping for fresh air, for freedom, for sunlight.

we don't have to go back, ever again. but we went, in spite of our fear, in spite of our awkwardness, hoping to find the courage to allow ourselves to be seen, to be loved, to be real. we have wanted connectedness, community, friends. we have wanted our daughter to believe in something beautiful and wild and personal. we have wanted that, too. we have wanted to believe that god is bigger than any church, yet sometimes he chooses to use them anyway.

we went in expecting a miracle, and came out believing the miracle is us.

as i sit by the lake, i feel the breeze cooling my face and brushing the hair away from my sticky skin. all is quiet and peaceful, except for the growl of a nearby tractor and the squeal of brakes from a passing car. squirrels play a frantic game of chase amidst the dying brown grass and crumpled leaves. the sound of chirping birds can barely be noticed over the din of a low-flying jet. were it not for the man-made intrusions into this place, it would be a scene of relaxation and pondering. as it is, however, i can hardly appreciate the loveliness of nature for the distractions.

my life is like this. a combination of the miraculous and the man-made, i struggle to find the beauty in the barren branches and clumps of dying grass. i seek quiet comfort and strength, yet i am distracted by others' expectations and their imposed definitions. though i strive for serenity and healing in the present, i am too often overwhelmed by the abuse of my past.

a duck, decorated with a green beak and green tail, floats serenely near the shore. he hardly notices the squealing of the tractor as it backs up, or the men in orange crawling the hill, picking up trash. he simply rides the current, dips his head in occasionally for a tasty snack, and floats contentedly on the top of the water.

i fight. i kick and scream and splash, impatiently expecting my life to suddenly make sense or become easier. what would it mean to let go of a part of my control? to ride the waves rather than conquer them? to let myself float rather than struggle to move?

these questions elude me. yet sitting here, in this place, i find that my shoulders have relaxed for the first time in weeks. the noises that seemed so intrusive and loud have faded to the whisper of the wind and the lapping of water. the cynicism i experienced just 45 minutes ago is replaced with wonder and marvel at the beauty of life and creation.

my life is still complicated. i still battle the demons of my past; memories still haunt me. yet i am discovering that despite the clutter of man-made intrusion, there can still be a peace, or a resolution, with the way things are; the good and lovely things which keep me breathing, keep me alive. through the beauty of the natural world, i can begin to glimpse a bit of the beauty within myself.

my prayers take tangible forms: stones, leaves, candles. i light candles late at night when the world is dark. i build stone altars on empty picnic tables, i crunch leaves in frustration. i use words, sometimes: scribble them frantically in notebooks, mumble them under my breath, sob them into my pillow in the depths of night.

i have connected god with people my entire life. from the earliest moments when i thought god hated me because my father said so, to more recent times when a friend tells me i am loved for the same reason, i have been unable to truly see god apart from humanity.

it has been a journey both toward and from, a journey of both holding on and daring to let go. kindness, abuse, threats, promises—all given by god, all offered through humans.

i have wanted to have a relationship with god that is separate, that is just me and something holy; a relationship that doesn't depend on the moods of people or their ability to be good. i think i am beginning to find the flickers of that. i am beginning to find the "i am" at the bottom of the abyss, the rope out of the chasm, a sense of presence in the midst of a lifetime of absence.

my connection with god, with something greater than myself, is slowly oozing into a shape, a definition; no longer a nebulous sense of something, but a knowing, a breathing, a presence in the room, sitting beside me. a presence independent of others, a presence independent of my behavior, a presence that sits with me and simply waits.

my faith is becoming.

through being real with my pain and honest with all that

lives within me, i am learning to risk.

some days it takes everything i have to keep believing.
some days i don't want to believe. some days i refuse to be
vulnerable, and i can only be honest.

some days i find myself lying in my bed unable to move.

"faith is the substance of things hoped for..."

god accepts me where i am.

where i am, in this moment, in this breath, in this moment
of existence, is still within god's love, still within god's
acceptance.

i am where i am, and god is bigger than me. god is bigger
than any person, than any definition from any person.
bigger than any person's cruelty or kindness. i am learning
to reach more toward god with every breath, and in that
reaching, and perhaps even through that reaching, i become
more able to believe.

i do believe. help thou, o god, my unbelief.

afterword

shortly after my father's last sexual assault against me, i testified before the state victim's witness program, and my case was approved. i received monetary compensation for my therapy bills; my therapist also received monetary compensation for his sessions with me at a lower-scaled fee. although the money didn't dramatically change my life (though it certainly helped), the fact that i was heard and believed and validated was life changing. that recognition was the beginning of my healing and freedom, a path i'm still on today. i have not seen nor spoken with any members of my family of origin for more than 12 years.

oh, and the meaning of my new name that my counselor gave me?

renée means "reborn."

thank you

my gratitude is offered to the following people:

- » **mark oestreicher, john raymond, jay howver, the emergentYS board**, and **zondervan** for believing in this book and honoring my story.
- » **bob carlton**, for presenting my book to Z, for friendship & shared stories, for god as mother, for grace.
- » **dave urbanski**, for your gentle editing hand and for your respect and kindness.
- » **jonathan green**, for your tender artistic treatment of my words.
- » **kate, geo, dar**, and **deb**, for walking through so much of my life with me, for laughter, for holding my hand, and for your continued friendship.
- » **doug**, for a decade of arduous therapy, for helping me find (and trust) my voice, and for my new name.
- » **jonfox, heidi, chris, deneice, rick, len, andy, jordon, christy (& darlene), dreama, mike, schock & family**, and many other bloggers and online friends who engage the conversation, hear my stories, and offer back their own.
- » **kathie**, for always believing.
- » **mark s.**, for the first freedom to disbelieve in god.
- » **andrew**, for psalm 88.

» **debbie**, for the laundry room.

» **cindi**, for giving me what i never knew of my mother and trusting her stories and her ashes to my care.

» **mark dowds**, for insight and confirmation.

» all of my **friends at "the office,"** for helping me believe i am loved.

» **karla**, for pelicans and dragon days; for northern lights.

» **larry**, for entering into my brokenness and caring about me even when i didn't know how to be cared for. you have been jesus in so many ways, and i am grateful for you.

» **george**, **carol**, **abby**, and **marty**, for being the family i never had, and for giving me a place among you.

» **david**, for filling my life with richness for which i can never find words; for poetry and story and myth; for the love of language, and for believing that i have "the gift."

» **eric** & **jordan**, for the redemption of your love, for being my family, for every moment you share your lives with me. i love you.

read more about the book and others' stories:
www.stumblingtowardfaith.com

share your stories with me:
renee@stumblingtowardfaith.com